GENOCIDE & PERSECUTION

Chile

Titles in the Genocide and Persecution Series

Afghanistan
Argentina
Armenia
Bosnia
Burma
Cambodia
Chile
Darfur
East Pakistan
El Salvador and Guatemala
The Holocaust
Indonesia
Kosovo
The Kurds
Liberia
Namibia
The People's Republic of China
The Romani
Russia
Rwanda
South Africa
Sri Lanka
Tibet
Uganda

Genocide & Persecution

Chile

David Erik Nelson
Book Editor

Frank Chalk
Consulting Editor

GREENHAVEN
PUBLISHING

Elizabeth Des Chenes, *Director, Content Strategy*
Cynthia Sanner, *Publisher*
Douglas Dentino, *Manager, New Product*

WCN: 01-100-101

For more information, contact:
Greenhaven Publishing, LLC
2544 Clinton Street
Buffalo NY 14224
Or you can visit our Internet site at http://greenhavenpublishing.com

LIBRARY OF CONGRESS CATALOGING-IN-PUBLICATION DATA

Chile / David Erik Nelson, book editor.
pages cm. -- (Genocide and persecution)
Includes bibliographical references and index.
ISBN 978-0-7377-6896-1 (hardcover)
1. Chile--History--Coup d'état, 1973. 2. Chile--History--1973-1988. 3. Pinochet Ugarte, Augusto. 4. Political persecution--Chile--History--20th century. 5. Human rights--Chile--History--20th century. 6. Crimes against humanity--Chile--History--20th century. I. Nelson, David Erik, editor of compilation.
F3100.C4367 2014
983.06'5--dc23 2013038408

Printed in the United States of America
1 2 3 4 5 6 7 18 17 16 15 14

Contents

Preface

> *"For the dead and the living, we must bear witness."*
>
> *Elie Wiesel, Nobel laureate and Holocaust survivor*

The histories of many nations are shaped by horrific events involving torture, violent repression, and systematic mass killings. The inhumanity of such events is difficult to comprehend, yet understanding why such events take place, what impact they have on society, and how they may be prevented in the future is vitally important. The Genocide and Persecution series provides readers with anthologies of previously published materials on acts of genocide, crimes against humanity, and other instances of extreme persecution, with an emphasis on events taking place in the twentieth and twenty-first centuries. The series offers essential historical background on these significant events in modern world history, presents the issues and controversies surrounding the events, and provides first-person narratives from people whose lives were altered by the events. By providing primary sources, as well as analysis of crucial issues, these volumes help develop critical-thinking skills and support global connections. In addition, the series directly addresses curriculum standards focused on informational text and literary nonfiction and explicitly promotes literacy in history and social studies.

Each Genocide and Persecution volume focuses on genocide, crimes against humanity, or severe persecution. Material from a variety of primary and secondary sources presents a multinational perspective on the event. Articles are carefully edited and introduced to provide context for readers. The series includes volumes on significant and widely studied events like the Holocaust, as well as events that are less often studied, such as the East Pakistan genocide in what is now Bangladesh. Some volumes focus on multiple events endured by a specific people, such as the Kurds, or multiple events enacted over time by a particular oppressor or in a particular location, such as the People's Republic of China.

Each volume is organized into three chapters. The first chapter provides readers with general background information and uses primary sources such as testimony from tribunals or international courts, documents or speeches from world leaders, and legislative text. The second chapter presents multinational perspectives on issues and controversies and addresses current implications or long-lasting effects of the event. Viewpoints explore such topics as root causes; outside interventions, if any; the impact on the targeted group and the region; and the contentious issues that arose in the aftermath. The third chapter presents first-person narratives from affected people, including survivors, family members of victims, perpetrators, officials, aid workers, and other witnesses.

In addition, numerous features are included in each volume of Genocide and Persecution:

- An annotated **table of contents** provides a brief summary of each essay in the volume.
- A **foreword** gives important background information on the recognition, definition, and study of genocide in recent history and examines current efforts focused on the prevention of future atrocities.
- A **chronology** offers important dates leading up to, during, and following the event.
- **Primary sources**—including historical newspaper accounts, testimony, and personal narratives—are among the varied selections in the anthology.
- **Illustrations**—including a world map, photographs, charts, graphs, statistics, and tables—are closely tied

to the text and chosen to help readers understand key points or concepts.

- **Sidebars**—including biographies of key figures and overviews of earlier or related historical events—offer additional content.
- **Pedagogical features**—including analytical exercises, writing prompts, and group activities—introduce each chapter and help reinforce the material. These features promote proficiency in writing, speaking, and listening skills and literacy in history and social studies.
- A **glossary** defines key terms, as needed.
- An annotated list of international **organizations to contact** presents sources of additional information on the volume topic.
- A **list of primary source documents** provides an annotated list of reports, treaties, resolutions, and judicial decisions related to the volume topic.
- A **for further research** section offers a bibliography of books, periodical articles, and Internet sources and an annotated section of other items such as films and websites.
- A comprehensive subject **index** provides access to key people, places, events, and subjects cited in the text.

The Genocide and Persecution series illuminates atrocities that cannot and should not be forgotten. By delving deeply into these events from a variety of perspectives, students and other readers are provided with the information they need to think critically about the past and its implications for the future.

Foreword

The term *genocide* often appears in news stories and other literature. It is not widely known, however, that the core meaning of the term comes from a legal definition, and the concept became part of international criminal law only in 1951 when the United Nations Convention on the Prevention and Punishment of the Crime of Genocide came into force. The word *genocide* appeared in print for the first time in 1944 when Raphael Lemkin, a Polish Jewish refugee from Adolf Hitler's World War II invasion of Eastern Europe, invented the term and explored its meaning in his pioneering book *Axis Rule in Occupied Europe*.

Humanity's Recognition of Genocide and Persecution

Lemkin understood that throughout the history of the human race there have always been leaders who thought they could solve their problems not only through victory in war, but also by destroying entire national, ethnic, racial, or religious groups. Such annihilations of entire groups, in Lemkin's view, deprive the world of the very cultural diversity and richness in languages, traditions, values, and practices that distinguish the human race from all other life on earth. Genocide is not only unjust, it threatens the very existence and progress of human civilization, in Lemkin's eyes.

Looking to the past, Lemkin understood that the prevailing coarseness and brutality of earlier human societies and the lower value placed on human life obscured the existence of genocide. Sacrifice and exploitation, as well as torture and public execution, had been common at different times in history. Looking toward a more humane future, Lemkin asserted the need to punish—and when possible prevent—a crime for which there had been no name until he invented it.

Legal Definitions of Genocide

On December 9, 1948, the United Nations adopted its Convention on the Prevention and Punishment of the Crime of Genocide (UNGC). Under Article II, genocide:

> means any of the following acts committed with intent to destroy, in whole or in part, a national, ethnical, racial or religious group, as such:
>
> (a) Killing members of the group;
>
> (b) Causing serious bodily or mental harm to members of the group;
>
> (c) Deliberately inflicting on the group conditions of life calculated to bring about its physical destruction in whole or in part;
>
> (d) Imposing measures intended to prevent births within the group;
>
> (e) Forcibly transferring children of the group to another group.

Article III of the convention defines the elements of the crime of genocide, making punishable:

> (a) Genocide;
>
> (b) Conspiracy to commit genocide;
>
> (c) Direct and public incitement to commit genocide;
>
> (d) Attempt to commit genocide;
>
> (e) Complicity in genocide.

After intense debate, the architects of the convention excluded acts committed with intent to destroy social, political, and economic groups from the definition of genocide. Thus, attempts to destroy whole social classes—the physically and mentally challenged, and homosexuals, for example—are not acts of genocide under the terms of the UNGC. These groups achieved a belated but very significant measure of protection under international criminal law in the Rome Statute of the International Criminal

Court, adopted at a conference on July 17, 1998, and entered into force on July 1, 2002.

The Rome Statute defined a crime against humanity in the following way:

> any of the following acts when committed as part of a widespread and systematic attack directed against any civilian population:
>
> (a) Murder;
>
> (b) Extermination;
>
> (c) Enslavement;
>
> (d) Deportation or forcible transfer of population;
>
> (e) Imprisonment or other severe deprivation of physical liberty in violation of fundamental rules of international law;
>
> (f) Torture;
>
> (g) Rape, sexual slavery, enforced prostitution, forced pregnancy, enforced sterilization, or any other form of sexual violence of comparable gravity;
>
> (h) Persecution against any identifiable group or collectivity on political, racial, national, ethnic, cultural, religious, gender . . . or other grounds that are universally recognized as impermissible under international law, in connection with any act referred to in this paragraph or any crime within the jurisdiction of this Court;
>
> (i) Enforced disappearance of persons;
>
> (j) The crime of apartheid;
>
> (k) Other inhumane acts of a similar character intentionally causing great suffering, or serious injury to body or to mental or physical health.

Although genocide is often ranked as "the crime of crimes," in practice prosecutors find it much easier to convict perpetrators of crimes against humanity rather than genocide under domestic laws. However, while Article I of the UNGC declares that countries adhering to the UNGC recognize genocide as "a crime under international law which they undertake to prevent and to punish," the Rome Statute provides no comparable international mechanism for the prosecution of crimes against humanity. A treaty would help individual countries and international institutions introduce measures to prevent crimes against humanity, as well as open more avenues to the domestic and international prosecution of war criminals.

The Evolving Laws of Genocide

In the aftermath of the serious crimes committed against civilians in the former Yugoslavia since 1991 and the Rwanda genocide of 1994, the United Nations Security Council created special international courts to bring the alleged perpetrators of these events to justice. While the UNGC stands as the standard definition of genocide in law, the new courts contributed significantly to today's nuanced meaning of genocide, crimes against humanity, ethnic cleansing, and serious war crimes in international criminal law.

Also helping to shape contemporary interpretations of such mass atrocity crimes are the special and mixed courts for Sierra Leone, Cambodia, Lebanon, and Iraq, which may be the last of their type in light of the creation of the International Criminal Court (ICC), with its broad jurisdiction over mass atrocity crimes in all countries that adhere to the Rome Statute of the ICC. The Yugoslavia and Rwanda tribunals have already clarified the law of genocide, ruling that rape can be prosecuted as a weapon in committing genocide, evidence of intent can be absent when convicting low-level perpetrators of genocide, and public incitement to commit genocide is a crime even if genocide does not immediately follow the incitement.

Several current controversies about genocide are worth noting and will require more research in the future:

1. Dictators accused of committing genocide or persecution may hold onto power more tightly for fear of becoming

vulnerable to prosecution after they step down. Therefore, do threats of international indictments of these alleged perpetrators actually delay transfers of power to more representative rulers, thereby causing needless suffering?

2. Would the large sum of money spent for international retributive justice be better spent on projects directly benefiting the survivors of genocide and persecution?
3. Can international courts render justice impartially or do they deliver only "victors' justice," that is the application of one set of rules to judge the vanquished and a different and laxer set of rules to judge the victors?

It is important to recognize that the law of genocide is constantly evolving, and scholars searching for the roots and early warning signs of genocide may prefer to use their own definitions of genocide in their work. While the UNGC stands as the standard definition of genocide in law, the debate over its interpretation and application will never end. The ultimate measure of the value of any definition of genocide is its utility for identifying the roots of genocide and preventing future genocides.

Motives for Genocide and Early Warning Signs

When identifying past cases of genocide, many scholars work with some version of the typology of motives published in 1990 by historian Frank Chalk and sociologist Kurt Jonassohn in their book *The History and Sociology of Genocide*. The authors identify the following four motives and acknowledge that they may overlap, or several lesser motives might also drive a perpetrator:

1. To eliminate a real or potential threat, as in Imperial Rome's decision to annihilate Carthage in 146 BC.
2. To spread terror among real or potential enemies, as in Genghis Khan's destruction of city-states and people who rebelled against the Mongols in the thirteenth century.

3. To acquire economic wealth, as in the case of the Massachusetts Puritans' annihilation of the native Pequot people in 1637.
4. To implement a belief, theory, or an ideology, as in the case of Germany's decision under Hitler and the Nazis to destroy completely the Jewish people of Europe from 1941 to 1945.

Although these motives represent differing goals, they share common early warning signs of genocide. A good example of genocide in recent times that could have been prevented through close attention to early warning signs was the genocide of 1994 inflicted on the people labeled as "Tutsi" in Rwanda. Between 1959 and 1963, the predominantly Hutu political parties in power stigmatized all Tutsi as members of a hostile racial group, violently forcing their leaders and many civilians into exile in neighboring countries through a series of assassinations and massacres. Despite systematic exclusion of Tutsi from service in the military, government security agencies, and public service, as well as systematic discrimination against them in higher education, hundreds of thousands of Tutsi did remain behind in Rwanda. Government-issued cards identified each Rwandan as Hutu or Tutsi.

A generation later, some Tutsi raised in refugee camps in Uganda and elsewhere joined together, first organizing politically and then militarily, to reclaim a place in their homeland. When the predominantly Tutsi Rwanda Patriotic Front invaded Rwanda from Uganda in October 1990, extremist Hutu political parties demonized all of Rwanda's Tutsi as traitors, ratcheting up hate propaganda through radio broadcasts on government-run Radio Rwanda and privately owned radio station RTLM. Within the print media, *Kangura* and other publications used vicious cartoons to further demonize Tutsi and to stigmatize any Hutu who dared advocate bringing Tutsi into the government. Massacres of dozens and later hundreds of Tutsi sprang up even as Rwandans prepared to elect a coalition government led by moderate political parties, and as the United Nations dispatched a small international military force led by Canadian general Roméo Dallaire to oversee the elections and political transition. Late in 1992, an international human rights organization's investigating team detected the hate propaganda campaign, verified systematic massacres of Tutsi, and warned the international community that Rwanda had already entered the early stages of genocide, to no avail. On April 6, 1994, Rwanda's genocidal killing accelerated at an alarming pace when someone shot down the airplane flying Rwandan president Juvenal Habyarimana home from peace talks in Arusha, Tanzania.

Hundreds of thousands of Tutsi civilians—including children, women, and the elderly—died horrible deaths because the world ignored the early warning signs of the genocide and refused to act. Prominent among those early warning signs were: 1) systematic, government-decreed discrimination against the Tutsi as members of a supposed racial group; 2) government-issued identity cards labeling every Tutsi as a member of a racial group; 3) hate propaganda casting all Tutsi as subversives and traitors; 4) organized assassinations and massacres targeting Tutsi; and 5) indoctrination of militias and special military units to believe that all Tutsi posed a genocidal threat to the existence of Hutu and would enslave Hutu if they ever again became the rulers of Rwanda.

Genocide Prevention and the Responsibility to Protect

The shock waves emanating from the Rwanda genocide forced world leaders at least to acknowledge in principle that the national sovereignty of offending nations cannot trump the responsibility of those governments to prevent the infliction of mass atrocities on their own people. When governments violate that obligation, the member states of the United Nations have a responsibility to get involved. Such involvement can take the form of, first, offering to help the local government change its ways through technical advice and development aid, and second—if the local government persists in assaulting its own people—initiating armed intervention to protect the civilians at risk. In 2005 the United Nations began to implement the Responsibility to Protect initiative, a framework of principles to guide the international community in preventing mass atrocities.

As in many real-world domains, theory and practice often diverge. Genocide and crimes against humanity are rooted in problems that produce failing states: poverty, poor education, extreme nationalism, lawlessness, dictatorship, and corruption. Implementing the principles of the Responsibility to Protect doctrine burdens intervening state leaders with the necessity of addressing each of those problems over a long period of time. And when those problems prove too intractable and complex to solve easily, the citizens of the intervening nations may lose patience, voting out the leader who initiated the intervention. Arguments based solely on humanitarian principles fail to overcome such concerns. What is needed to persuade political leaders to stop preventable mass atrocities are compelling arguments based on their own national interests.

Preventable mass atrocities threaten the national interests of all states in five specific ways:

1. Mass atrocities create conditions that engender widespread and concrete threats from terrorism, piracy, and other forms of lawlessness on the land and sea;
2. Mass atrocities facilitate the spread of warlordism, whose tentacles block affordable access to vital raw materials produced in the affected country and threaten the prosperity of all nations that depend on the consumption of these resources;
3. Mass atrocities trigger cascades of refugees and internally displaced populations that, combined with climate change and growing international air travel, will accelerate the worldwide incidence of lethal infectious diseases;

4. Mass atrocities spawn single-interest parties and political agendas that drown out more diverse political discourse in the countries where the atrocities take place and in the countries that host large numbers of refugees. Xenophobia and nationalist backlashes are the predictable consequences of government indifference to mass atrocities elsewhere that could have been prevented through early actions;
5. Mass atrocities foster the spread of national and transnational criminal networks trafficking in drugs, women, arms, contraband, and laundered money.

Alerting elected political representatives to the consequences of mass atrocities should be part of every student movement's agenda in the twenty-first century. Adam Smith, the great political economist and author of *The Wealth of Nations*, put it best when he wrote: "It is not from the benevolence of the butcher, the brewer, or the baker that we expect our dinner, but from their regard to their own interest." Self-interest is a powerful engine for good in the marketplace and can be an equally powerful motive and source of inspiration for state action to prevent genocide and mass persecution. In today's new global village, the lives we save may be our own.

Frank Chalk

Frank Chalk, who has a doctorate from the University of Wisconsin-Madison, is a professor of history and director of the Montreal Institute for Genocide and Human Rights Studies at Concordia University in Montreal, Canada. He is coauthor, with Kurt

Jonassohn, of The History and Sociology of Genocide *(1990); coauthor with General Roméo Dallaire, Kyle Matthews, Carla Barqueiro, and Simon Doyle of* Mobilizing the Will to Intervene: Leadership to Prevent Mass Atrocities *(2010); and associate editor of the three-volume Macmillan Reference USA* Encyclopedia of Genocide and Crimes Against Humanity *(2004). Chalk served as president of the International Association of Genocide Scholars from June 1999 to June 2001. His current research focuses on the use of radio and television broadcasting in the incitement and prevention of genocide, and domestic laws on genocide. For more information on genocide and examples of the experiences of people displaced by genocide and other human rights violations, interested readers can consult the websites of the Montreal Institute for Genocide and Human Rights Studies (http://migs.concordia.ca) and the Montreal Life Stories project (www.lifestoriesmontreal.ca).*

World Map

Greenland (Denmark)
Alaska (U.S.)
CANADA
UNITED STATES
ATLANTIC OCEAN
Azores Islands (Portugal)
Hawaii (U.S.)
Tropic of Cancer
MEXICO
see inset below
PACIFIC OCEAN
CAPE VERDE
French Guiana (France)
Galápagos Islands (Ecuador)
COLOMBIA
SURINAME
Equator
Line Islands (U.S.)
ECUADOR
American Samoa (U.S.)
PERU
BRAZIL
SAMOA
BOLIVIA
French Polynesia (France)
TONGA
Tropic of Capricorn
PARAGUAY
Pitcairn Islands (U.K.)
CHILE
URUGUAY
ARGENTINA
Falkland Islands (U.K.)
Antarctic Circle
SOUTHERN OCEAN
160°W
140°W
120°W
100°W
80°W
60°W
40°W
80°N
60°N
40°N
20°N
0°
20°S
40°S
60°S
80°S
Gulf of Mexico
UNITED STATES
N
BAHAMAS
Tropic of Cancer
Turks and Caicos Islands (U.K.)
CUBA
U.S. Virgin Islands (U.S.)
British Virgin Islands (U.K.)
Anguilla (U.K.)
St. Martin (St. Maarten) (France & Neth. Antilles)
ANTIGUA AND BARBUDA
MEXICO
HAITI
Cayman Islands (U.K.)
Puerto Rico (U.S.)
ST. KITTS AND NEVIS
Montserrat (U.K.)
Guadeloupe (France)
DOMINICA
BELIZE
JAMAICA
DOMINICAN REPUBLIC
GUATEMALA
Martinique (France)
HONDURAS
Caribbean Sea
ST. LUCIA
BARBADOS
EL SALVADOR
ST. VINCENT AND THE GRENADINES
GRENADA
NICARAGUA
0 200 400 mi.
0 200 400 km
Aruba (Neth.)
Netherlands Antilles (Neth.)
TRINIDAD AND TOBAGO
COSTA RICA
Lake Maracaibo
VENEZUELA
PACIFIC OCEAN
PANAMA
COLOMBIA
GUYANA
90°W
85°W
80°W
75°W
60°W
25°N
20°N
15°N
10°N

ARCTIC OCEAN
see inset below
Arctic Circle
ICELAND
RUSSIA
KAZAKHSTAN
MONGOLIA
GEORGIA
AZER.
UZBEK.
KYRGYZSTAN
TURKMEN.
TAJIKISTAN
ARMENIA
NORTH KOREA
SOUTH KOREA
JAPAN
CHINA
MOROCCO
ISRAEL
IRAQ
IRAN
AFGHAN.
JORDAN
KUWAIT
BAHRAIN
QATAR
PAKISTAN
NEPAL
BHUTAN
ALGERIA
LIBYA
EGYPT
SAUDI ARABIA
U.A.E.
OMAN
INDIA
BANGLADESH
MYANMAR (BURMA)
LAOS
TAIWAN (Claimed by China)
PACIFIC OCEAN
CHAD
SUDAN
ERITREA
YEMEN
DJIBOUTI
ETHIOPIA
SOMALIA
THAILAND
VIETNAM
CAMBODIA
PHILIPPINES
SRI LANKA
MARSHALL ISLANDS
CEN. AFR. REP.
CAMEROON
BRUNEI
MALAYSIA
FEDERATED STATES OF MICRONESIA
KIRIBATI
see inset below
DEM. REP. OF THE CONGO
UGANDA
KENYA
MALDIVES
SINGAPORE
INDONESIA
NAURU
SÃO TOMÉ AND PRÍNCIPE
GABON
CONGO
RWANDA
BURUNDI
TANZANIA
SEYCHELLES
TIMOR-LESTE
PAPUA NEW GUINEA
SOLOMON ISLANDS
TUVALU
ATLANTIC OCEAN
ANGOLA
MALAWI
ZAMBIA
COMOROS
INDIAN OCEAN
MOZAMBIQUE
VANUATU
FIJI ISLANDS
MADAGASCAR
MAURITIUS
ZIMBABWE
BOTSWANA
NAMIBIA
Réunion (France)
New Caledonia (France)
AUSTRALIA
SWAZILAND
SOUTH AFRICA
LESOTHO
0 1000 2000 mi.
0 1000 2000 km
N
NEW ZEALAND
SOUTHERN OCEAN
ANTARCTICA
Western Sahara (Morocco)
ALGERIA
MAURITANIA
MALI
NIGER
SENEGAL
GAMBIA
GUINEA-BISSAU
GUINEA
BURKINA FASO
BENIN
SIERRA LEONE
TOGO
NIGERIA
ATLANTIC OCEAN
CÔTE D'IVOIRE
GHANA
LIBERIA
0 200 400 mi.
0 200 400 km
Gulf of Guinea
EQUATORIAL GUINEA
SWEDEN
FINLAND
NORWAY
0 200 400 mi.
0 200 400 km
ESTONIA
North Sea
RUSSIA
IRELAND
UNITED KINGDOM
DENMARK
LATVIA
Baltic Sea
LITHUANIA
RUSSIA
NETHERLANDS
BELARUS
POLAND
GERMANY
ATLANTIC OCEAN
BELGIUM
LUX.
CZECH REP.
UKRAINE
SLOVAKIA
LIECH.
Bay of Biscay
FRANCE
SWITZ.
AUSTRIA
MOLDOVA
HUNGARY
SLOVENIA
ROMANIA
CROATIA
ANDORRA
MONACO
ITALY
BOS. AND HERZ.
SERBIA
Black Sea
PORTUGAL
SAN MARINO
MONT.
BULGARIA
SPAIN
Corsica (France)
Sardinia (Italy)
ALBANIA
MAC.
VATICAN CITY
TURKEY
Gibraltar (U.K.)
Ceuta (Spain)
Melilla (Spain)
Balearic Islands (Spain)
Sicily (Italy)
GREECE
MALTA
Mediterranean Sea
CYPRUS
SYRIA
MOROCCO
ALGERIA
TUNISIA
Crete (Greece)
LEBANON

Chronology

November 4, 1970 Supported by a broad coalition of Communists and Socialists, Salvador Allende takes office as the world's first democratically elected Marxist president.

August 24, 1973 President Allende appoints General Augusto Pinochet as commander-in-chief of the Chilean army.

September 11, 1973 The Chilean military stages a coup, taking control of Chile. Allende is killed while being taken prisoner, likely from a self-inflicted gunshot wound (although this is disputed).

Late 1973 The ruling military junta suspends the constitution, dissolves congress, bans opposition parties and trade unions, and takes control of Chile's media.

December 17, 1974 The military junta formally transfers power to General Pinochet, declaring him president.

April 1978 President Pinochet declares a general amnesty for anyone involved in human rights abuses since the military coup.

September 11, 1980 Chile ratifies a new constitution by way of a highly controversial public referendum.

October 5, 1988 Pinochet loses a public referendum, also called a "plebiscite," on whether

	he should continue to rule Chile with 56 percent of the population voting "no."
December 14, 1989	Patricio Aylwin defeats Pinochet in open elections. Aylwin takes office on March 11, 1990, while Pinochet remains commander-in-chief of the army.
February 1991	Chile's National Commission for Truth and Reconciliation publishes the Rettig Report, which indicated that almost three thousand people were killed by political violence or "disappeared" under Pinochet.
March 1998	Pinochet retires as commander-in-chief and is immediately sworn in as senator-for-life (granting him lifetime immunity from prosecution for atrocities committed under his regime).
Late 1998–early 1999	While in London for surgery Pinochet is arrested for possible involvement in the torture and disappearance of Spanish citizens during his regime. Pinochet is ultimately found to be unfit for extradition and trial, and he is returned to Chile.
2000	Chilean judges strip Pinochet of his immunity, but he cannot stand trial due to poor health.
December 10, 2006	Pinochet dies of congestive heart failure, having never answered for any of roughly three hundred counts of human rights violations, tax evasion, and embezzlement brought against him.

CHAPTER 1

Historical Background on Chile Under Augusto Pinochet

Chapter Exercises

STATISTICS

	Chile
Total Area	756,102 sq km (291,933 sq mi) World ranking: 38
Population	17,216,945 (July 2013 estimate) World ranking: 62
Ethnic Groups	White and white-Amerindian 95.4%, Mapuche 4%, other indigenous groups 0.6% (2002 census)
Religions	Roman Catholic 70%, Evangelical 15.1%, Jehovah's Witnesses 1.1%, other Christian 1%, other 4.6%, none 8.3% (2002 census)
Literacy (total population)	95.7% Average years of education: 15 years
GDP	$319.4 billion (2012 estimate); $18 billion (1973) Current World ranking: 43 United States' GDP: $1,566 billion (2012 estimate); $1,369 billion (1973) Current World ranking: 1
Political Parties	Broad Social Movement or MAS, Citizen Left or IC, Equality Party, National Renewal or RN, Independent Democratic Union or UDI, Christian Democratic Party or PDC, Party for Democracy or PPD, Radical Social Democratic Party or PRSD, Socialist Party or PS, Communist Party of Chile (Partido Comunista de Chile) or PC, Ecological Green Party, Humanist Party or PH, Independent Regionalist Party or PRI, Progressive Party or PRO.

Source: *The World Factbook*. Washington, DC: Central Intelligence Agency, 2013. www.cia.gov.

1. Analyzing Statistics

Question 1: Compare Chile's gross domestic product (GDP) today and in 1973 (the year of Augusto Pinochet's military coup). By what percentage has GDP changed? By what percentage did the US GDP change over the same period? To what degree may economic conditions have contributed to the military coup? Did the military junta improve the economy, or did an improving economy make it possible for citizens to return their country to a functional democracy?

Question 2: Genocide is often characterized as arising from tensions between ethnic or religious groups. Does Chile seem very ethnically or racially diverse? Does the population appear to have adequate access to education? Does this seem like a nation you would expect to descend into chaotic upheaval and genocide? Why or why not?

Question 3: How many political parties are there in Chile? Is this greater or fewer than the number of parties in Chile in 1973? How does it compare to the United States? Does this level of political diversity have any bearing on Chile's stability?

2. Writing Prompt

Write an article describing conditions in the national stadium shortly after the 1973 military coup. Give your article a compelling title and work both to inform readers of the facts of the event (who, what, when, where, and why) as well as elicit an emotional response.

3. Group Activity

Break into small groups randomly assigned to be sympathetic to either Salvador Allende's Communist/Socialist government or the military coup and Pinochet's regime. Given the current state of Chile as an admired democracy with a strong economy, were the extreme measures used in the past justifiable? Why or why not?

Viewpoint 1

An Overview of Pinochet's Military Coup in Chile

Peter Kornbluh

In the following viewpoint, the author gives a concise overview of Augusto Pinochet's political career, including his part in Chile's violent 1973 military coup and his central role in human rights violations attributed to his regime. After Pinochet left office, Chilean and international prosecutors spent sixteen years attempting to bring the former dictator to justice. Nonetheless, upon his death in December of 2006, Augusto Pinochet had never stood trial for crimes against humanity. Peter Kornbluh is director of the Chile Documentation Project at the National Security Archive. The project seeks to collect and publish declassified government documents regarding US intervention in Chile and the Pinochet regime. Kornbluh is author of several books examining US foreign policy including The Pinochet File: A Declassified Dossier on Atrocity and Accountability *and* Low Intensity Warfare: How the USA Fights Wars Without Declaring Them.

Peter Kornbluh, "Pinochet, Augusto," *Encyclopedia of Genocide and Crimes Against Humanity,* vol. 2. Detroit: Macmillan Reference USA, 2005, pp. 805–809.

Recognized as one of the most ruthless and violent strongmen in the history of Latin America, General Augusto Pinochet's name became synonymous with human rights atrocities during the last quarter of the twentieth century. During his seventeen-year military regime in Chile, his security forces were responsible for the murders of 3,197 Chilean citizens. Of those, 1,100 were "disappeared"—abused to death and buried in still-secret graves, or thrown from military helicopters into the Pacific Ocean. An estimated 30,000 Chileans survived imprisonment and severe torture by agents of Pinochet's secret police—electric shock, beatings, near-drowning, and rape in secret detention facilities. In the mid-1970s, the Pinochet regime also organized a network of secret police agencies (given the code name Operation Condor) that coordinated the repression of groups and individuals who had been identified as opponents of the military governments of the Southern Cone (Argentina, Brazil, Chile, Paraguay, and Uruguay). Condor's methods included secret surveillance, kidnapping, interrogation, torture, and terrorist attacks. International efforts to hold General Pinochet legally accountable for human rights atrocities in Chile and acts of terrorism abroad led to his arrest for crimes against humanity in London in 1998.

Officials of Scotland Yard detained Pinochet on October 16, 1998, while he was recovering from back surgery at a private London hospital. He was served with an arrest warrant filed through Interpol by Spanish judges seeking to extradite him to Madrid to stand trial for "crimes of genocide and terrorism." For more than five hundred days, Pinochet was kept under house arrest in England; legal proceedings against him became a cause célèbre around the world. His detention became a leading symbol of the globalization of justice, and elevated and transformed the principle of universal jurisdiction—the ability of the international community to pursue the prosecution of dictators, torturers, and mass murderers beyond the borders of their home nations—into a precedent for future legal efforts against perpetrators of human rights crimes.

Young opponents of the Augusto Pinochet regime are arrested on November 23, 1979, just days after the military coup in Chile that placed Pinochet in power. © Keystone-France/Gamma-Keystone via Getty Images.

Pinochet's Violent Rise to Power

General Augusto Pinochet took power on September 11, 1973, during a U.S.-supported bloody military coup that overthrew the democratically elected Popular Unity government of Salvador Allende. In a country that had a long tradition of civility and constitutional rule, the military takeover was brutal and violent.

In the six weeks that followed the coup approximately 1,500 civilians were killed, including some 320 to 360 who were summarily executed, according to U.S. intelligence reports. More than 13,500 Chilean citizens and several thousand foreigners were detained through mass arrests and sent to detention camps. Many of those were brought to Chile's National Stadium, which was transformed from a sports arena into a center for interrogation, torture, and execution. Two U.S. citizens, Charles Horman and Frank Teruggi, were among the hundreds who were killed there.

Born on November 25, 1915, Pinochet entered the military academy in Santiago at age seventeen and rose steadily through the ranks of the Chilean army over the forty years that followed. In late August 1973, he succeeded General Carlos Prats as Commander-in-Chief of the Army. In the months leading up to the coup Prats opposed the overthrow of the elected government; his forced resignation and his replacement by Pinochet enabled coup-plotting to accelerate.

As head of the powerful Chilean army, Pinochet outmaneuvered other commanders of the Chilean Armed Forces who had expected to govern Chile after the coup by way of a rotating leadership within the military junta. In June 1974 Pinochet pressured the other members of the junta to name him "Supreme Chief of the Nation." On December 18, 1974, he decreed himself "President of the Republic"—a title he kept until early 1990, when he was forced to yield power to a new civilian government.

Ruling a Nation Through Systemic Torture and Murder

During his seventeen-year rule, Chile became a pariah state, internationally condemned for ongoing, systematic violations of human rights. Pinochet played a leadership role in initiating and overseeing many of these atrocities. One month after the coup, he authorized a death squad, led by his close associate General Sergio Arellano, to "expedite justice" in relation to civic, leaders of the former Allende government—police chiefs, mayors, local union officials—who had been arrested in the northern provinces after the coup. Using a Puma helicopter, a five-member military team led by General Arellano flew to various northern cities and, at each stop, selected prisoners and shot or bayoneted them in the middle of the night. Over a period of four days, sixty-eight civilians were killed, having committed no crime other than serving in local community leadership roles under the elected Allende government. This series of atrocities became known as "the Caravan of Death."

Members of the caravan team were subsequently integrated into a new secret police force known as the Directorate of National Intelligence (DINA). Pinochet handpicked Colonel Manuel Contreras, a close friend of his in the Chilean military with no background in intelligence, to be director of DINA. United States intelligence reports described Contreras as a "strong character, with intense loyalty to President Pinochet. . . . [H]e will advance only with the personal support of President Pinochet." Between 1974 and 1977 DINA expanded into a massive, institutionalized force of repression in Chile, terrorizing Chilean society at every level. DINA agents conducted clandestine raids and arrests; it forced prisoners through a network of clandestine interrogation centers to extract information from them. Many DINA prisoners were tortured to death and then "disappeared." The U.S. military reported from Santiago that DINA was "becoming a modern day Gestapo." One informant announced to U.S. officials, "There are three sources of power in Chile: Pinochet, God, and DINA."

DINA served as the central pillar of Pinochet's power. It actively eliminated all leftist opposition to his regime in Chile, and Contreras assigned agents to spy on other military commanders and intimidate anyone who challenged Pinochet's authority. Through executive decrees Pinochet bestowed on DINA the authority to establish a virtual monopoly over repression in Chile. Officially, DINA fell under the jurisdiction of the military junta. In reality, Contreras reported only to—and only took orders from—

General Pinochet. Contreras met with Pinochet every morning, at 7:30 A.M., to brief him on DINA operations. United States intelligence agents reported: "The President issues instructions on DINA: is aware of its activities; and, in fact, heads it."

Pinochet Coordinated International Terrorist Attacks

Pinochet's secret police not only carried out vicious acts of repression at home, but also sought to dispose of opponents of his regime abroad. In September 1974 DINA agents, using a car bomb, assassinated General Prats (Pinochet's predecessor as Commander-in-Chief of the army) who was living in exile in Buenos Aires, Argentina. The bomb also killed Prats's wife. A year later, DINA agents orchestrated the shooting of a leader of the Chilean Christian Democratic Party and his wife in Rome, Italy. In November 1975 Colonel Contreras decided to coordinate efforts with the military regimes of other Southern Cone countries to track down and eliminate dissidents in exile; he invited intelligence officials from Argentina, Paraguay, Uruguay, and Bolivia to come to Santiago and establish what he called an "Interpol against subversion in Latin America." This network of military intelligence services (the aforementioned Operation Condor) carried out violent, clandestine acts of terror in the region and throughout the world for more than five years.

Operation Condor quickly became the most sinister state-sponsored terrorist network in the Western Hemisphere, if not the world. In coordination with neighboring military governments, the Pinochet regime implemented surveillance, kidnappings, brutal interrogations, and the secret detention of political opponents in the Southern Cone, Europe, and even the United States. United States intelligence agencies eventually learned that "a third and reportedly very secret phase of 'Operation Condor' involves the formation of special teams from member countries who are to carry out operations to include assassinations." In September 1976, with the assistance of Paraguay, agents of DINA traveled to the United States to undertake what has become the best known Condor plot: the car-bombing assassination of Pinochet's leading critic-in-exile, former Chilean Ambassador Orlando Letelier. That September 21, 1976, car bombing in downtown Washington, D.C., also took the life of Letelier's colleague, 25-year-old Ronni Karpen Moffitt, and was considered at the time to be the most egregious act of international terrorism to ever have taken place in the U.S. capital. Within a week of the assassination, the FBI reported that it had probably been the work of Operation Condor.

In the spring of 1978, when the U.S. Justice Department presented the Chilean military government with clear evidence of DINA's role in the car bombing, General Pinochet personally took the lead in covering up the crime and obstructing U.S. efforts to bring those guilty to justice. The CIA learned that Pinochet was pursuing a multifaceted plan to derail the investigation, which included protecting DINA director Manuel Contreras from prosecution; stalling on U.S. requests for evidence; tampering with witnesses—Pinochet ordered one member of the assassination team who wanted to turn himself over to the FBI to "stay at his post"; and intervening with the Chilean Supreme Court to assure that neither Contreras nor his subordinates would be extradited to Washington. Pinochet, the CIA reported, "has manipulated the Supreme Court judges and now is satisfied that the court will reject extradition of any Chileans indicted."

Up to the point of the Letelier-Moffitt assassination, General Pinochet had enjoyed positive relations with the United States. In a private meeting in June 1976, Secretary of State Henry Kissinger said to Pinochet: "[I]n the United States, as you know, we are sympathetic with what you are trying to do here. . . . We want to help, not undermine, you." After the assassination, however, President Jimmy Carter held Pinochet at arms length and openly pressed the regime to improve its human rights record. Initially, the Reagan administration supported General Pinochet as a forceful anticommunist ally and

CHILE
N
PERU
BRAZIL
BOLIVIA
Arica
Iquique
Antofagasta
PARAGUAY
SOUTH PACIFIC OCEAN
Copiapó
La Serena
ARGENTINA
Valparaíso
Santiago
Rancagua
URUGUAY
Talca
Concepción
Temuco
Valdivia
Puerto Montt
SOUTH ATLANTIC OCEAN
Coihaique
Provincial Capital
National Capital
Punta Arenas

a kindred spirit in the furtherance of free-market economic policies. But by the mid-1980s, when the Chilean economy suffered a severe recession and the left wing of that nation began to reemerge as a significant political force despite continuing repression, the United States moved to support what the State Department called a "real and orderly transition to democracy."

Pinochet Reluctantly Permits Chile to Return to Democracy

In an effort to extend his dictatorship through to the end of the twentieth century, Pinochet called a plebiscite for October 1988. If a majority of Chileans voted "No" (to Pinochet), new elections would be held in 1989 and the military would turn over power to a civilian president. Although Pinochet expected to win, he developed a contingency plan that would go into effect if it appeared that he was losing. "Close supporters of President Pinochet are said to have contingency plans to derail the plebiscite by encouraging and staging acts of violence," one top-secret U.S. intelligence report stated.

Pinochet would then institute a state of emergency and declare the election "invalid." When his own commanders failed to implement that plan on the day of the plebiscite, Pinochet attempted to get the rest of the junta to authorize the use of the armed forces to seize the capital and nullify the election. The junta refused. The campaign of "No" won.

General Pinochet turned over the presidency to a civilian leader, Patricio Aylwin, on March 11, 1990. Yet, he retained his powerful position as commander of the Chilean armed forces, a post from which he commanded the new civilian government not to pursue any prosecution of the human rights crimes that had been committed under his regime. "The day they touch one of my men the state of law ends," he warned. When Pinochet finally stepped down from the military command, in March 1998, he assumed the title of *Senador Vitalica* (Senator for Life), providing himself with additional legal immunity from prosecution inside Chile.

Early judicial cases filed against Pinochet by the families of his victims failed to overcome the legal obstacles his regime had imposed on the Chilean court system. Internationally, however, other avenues were being explored. In 1996, in Madrid, Joan Garcés, a Spanish lawyer and former aide to Salvador Allende, filed a criminal case with a special branch of the Spanish judiciary called the *Audiencia National,* which accepted the principle of universal jurisdiction for offenses such as genocide, terrorism, and other crimes against humanity. For two years, however, Spanish authorities had no way of physically securing the target of their investigation. After Pinochet traveled to London on September 21, 1998, however, Garcés arranged for judge Baltazar Garzón to send a detention request to Scotland Yard, under the European Anti-Terrorism Convention. A British magistrate signed an arrest warrant for Pinochet on October 16; late that evening, Scotland Yard detectives secured his room at the private London clinic where he was recuperating from back surgery, disarmed his bodyguards, and served him with a "priority red warrant" for crimes against humanity.

Challenges to Prosecuting Pinochet

The saga of Pinochet's arrest in London lasted sixteen months and caught the attention of the world community. His case was unprecedented: a former head of state detained outside his homeland for extradition to a third country. Already a recognized symbol of human rights atrocities, Pinochet became the leading symbol of the globalization of justice for perpetrators of such crimes. His arrest fostered hopes for many of his victims and their families that they might finally face him in a court of law. And the international effort to bring him to justice paved a legal path for similar prosecutions against other former dictators and military commanders accused of human rights crimes.

Pinochet lost all legal battles in Britain to prevent his extradition to Madrid. But behind-the-scenes political lobbying by the Chilean government, which found itself under intense pressure from the military to obtain Pinochet's release, and the resistance of José Aznar, the conservative Spanish prime minister who opposed Judge Garzón's effort to prosecute Pinochet in Madrid, appeared to convince British authorities to let Pinochet go. On March 2, 2000, British Home Secretary Jack Straw ruled that Pinochet had suffered a stroke that had resulted in mild dementia and therefore would be released on humanitarian grounds.

Pinochet returned to Chile the next day, believing himself to be finally free of legal threats. Within three days of his return, however, Chilean Judge Juan Guzman filed a legal request to have Pinochet's immunity lifted so that he could be prosecuted for disappearances associated with the Caravan of Death atrocities. On May 23, 2000, Chile's Court of Appeals surprised Chileans and the international community by voting to strip Pinochet of his immunity; the Chilean Supreme Court upheld that decision on June 5. In December, Judge Guzman indicted Pinochet as the "intellectual author" of the Caravan of Death; and in early 2001, for the first time, Pinochet was actually interrogated about his knowledge of and role in those crimes.

But, just as the British had released Pinochet on health grounds, eventually the Chilean courts yielded to the arguments of Pinochet's lawyers that he was "mentally unfit due to dementia" and therefore unable to stand trial for the murders and disappearances in the Caravan case. Pinochet then issued a statement that he was retiring from political life. "I have a clean conscience," he said. "The work of my government will be judged by history."

At age eighty-eight, Pinochet did not retire quietly. In November 2003 he gave an interview to the Spanish language television network *Telemundo,* in which he described himself "as a good angel" who should be thanked for his contributions to Chile. Citing Pinochet's lucidity during the interview, Judge

Guzman again petitioned the courts, to strip Pinochet of his immunity—this time to prosecute him for murders relating to Operation Condor. On May 28, 2004, a Chilean court ruled that Pinochet could indeed stand trial for these crimes against humanity. While it remained likely that Pinochet would still escape justice through a decision of the Chilean Supreme Court to block his prosecution, the Condor case assured that he would not evade the verdict of history. [Pinochet died of congestive heart failure on December 10, 2006, never having stood trial for any crimes against humanity.]

VIEWPOINT 2

Augusto Pinochet: Villain to Some, Hero to Others

Tom Gjelten

The following viewpoint was originally broadcast on US radio the day of Augusto Pinochet's death, December 10, 2006. It highlights the violence of his coup and ensuing regime, as well as the deeply mixed feelings of the Chilean people. More than a third of all Chileans supported Pinochet's leadership throughout his rule. While he may be admired for policies that transformed the Chilean economy—often called the "Chilean Miracle"—the viewpoint states that Pinochet's true legacy is as a test case in international law. Tom Gjelten has been a correspondent for National Public Radio for over three decades. He is the author or coauthor of several books including Professionalism in War Reporting: A Correspondent's View *and* Crimes of War: What the Public Should Know.

General Augusto Pinochet, who ruled Chile as a dictator for 17 years, is dead. He led the military coup that overthrew Chile's elected socialist president, Salvador Allende, in 1973. He was ruthless in eliminating his political opponents in Chile, and ultimately was held responsible for the torture and deaths of thousands of people.

Augusto Pinochet Ugarte was a disciplined soldier in a country where the military normally obeyed civilian rule. Even when other army officers began grumbling about Chile's left-wing president, Salvador Allende, Pinochet continued to follow the president's orders. In June 1973, Allende appointed Pinochet commander-in-chief of the Chilean Armed Forces.

Ariel Dorfman is a Chilean writer who once worked for Allende. He remembers answering the phone in Allende's office when Pinochet called.

"I said, 'Just a moment please. I'll find him. I'll find him,'" Dorfman says, "because I thought this is ours, this is Pinochet, he's our guy."

But in the end he was not the president's guy.

Allende was implementing socialist economic policies in Chile, with disastrous results. Gen. Pinochet finally agreed with other military officers that they had to stop Allende, and from that point on, Pinochet showed him no mercy.

On Sept. 11, 1973, he ordered a fierce ground and air assault on the presidential palace. In a recorded radio communication that day, Pinochet discussed the attack with Vice Admiral Patricio Carvajal, a fellow coup plotter. Carvajal had been in touch with Allende, who was holed up in the palace, and he relayed a message that Allende wanted to talk.

Pinochet interrupts him, shouting, "Unconditional surrender! No negotiation! Unconditional surrender!"

"Right," Carvajal says. He then suggests that Allende be guaranteed only passage out of the country. Pinochet agrees, but then makes a joke that suggests he may just as soon see Allende dead.

"He can be flown out of the country," Pinochet says, "but then, old boy, while he's flying, the airplane falls out of the sky."

As it turned out, Allende was never put on a plane. Surrounded and under attack, he shot himself in the head rather than surrender to Pinochet's forces.

In the days that followed, Pinochet's security forces rounded up Allende supporters wherever they could find them. Many were tortured. More than 3,000 were killed or disappeared. One hundred thousand Allende supporters went into exile.

Ariel Dorfman, who fled to the United States, thinks Pinochet concluded that once he launched his brutal crackdown, he had no option but to go all the way.

"When you begin with that level of violence, I think the fear that is generated inside people like Pinochet forces them to continue a reign of terror that will not stop because it's the only way in which you can silence the voices," Dorfman says. "Remember that Allende had received 45 percent of the vote in the previous election. That's an enormous amount of people to repress."

Pinochet's reach extended beyond Chile. Evidence has tied his secret police to an assassination in Argentina, an attempted assassination in Rome, and to a car bombing in downtown Washington, D.C., in 1976. A former Chilean diplomat and his American assistant were killed in that attack; U.S. officials judged it an act of state-sponsored terrorism.

And yet in Chile, as much as one-third of the population stood with Pinochet to the end. Fernando Alessandri, whose family has a long political lineage in Chile, says that the Pinochet he remembers from his youth was not the evil figure portrayed by Pinochet opponents.

"He lived a block and a half away from where we lived, so I got to see him jogging every morning at 6," Alessandri says. "He was a man that had a profound love for his country. He was an authoritarian—a leader."

Alessandri's grandfather, Jorge Alessandri, narrowly lost the 1970 presidential election to Salvador Allende and subsequently supported Pinochet's coup against Allende.

So did the United States. Having undermined the Allende government, U.S. officials were quick to praise Pinochet when he brought in American economic advisers and instituted radical free-market reforms in Chile.

But Pinochet's brutality and stubbornness soon proved too much even for his allies. Elliott Abrams, the assistant secretary of

Augusto Pinochet participates in a September 11, 1997, ceremony marking the anniversary of the military coup that brought him to power in 1973. © Chris Bouroncle/AFP/Getty Images.

The Corrupt Dictator

For much of his career, General Pinochet maintained the image of the incorruptible, if ruthlessly violent, Prussian-style officer. But in July 2004, a financial scandal shattered his carefully honed image as an austere, modest, professional solider—a reputation that had distinguished Pinochet's career from other Latin American strongmen who were known as much for their greed as their expressions.

A US Senate Committee, investigating money laundering and foreign corruption at the Washington DC–based Riggs National Bank, uncovered detailed documentation on secret bank accounts Pinochet maintained outside of Chile after he was forced from power in 1990. The Senate investigation revealed that Riggs [had] opened multiple accounts for Pinochet and "deliberately assisted him in the concealment and movement of his funds while he was under investigation [in London] and the subject of a worldwide court order freezing his assets."

Pinochet's Chilean tax returns record an official income of $90,000 a year. But between 1994 and 2002, he deposited up to $8 million into three personal and three shell corporation accounts created by Riggs officials to hide his wealth. During his long detention under house arrest in London, he drew on these

state for Latin America under President Reagan, says that he and other U.S. officials grew increasingly frustrated over Pinochet's unwillingness to return Chile to democracy.

"By the mid-80s, it was clear that he had outlived any usefulness he had ever had," Abrams says. "Even if you thought he was terrific in 1973, by 1983, it was time for him to go."

But Pinochet paid no heed to any such complaints. On the tenth anniversary of his coup, as on the previous nine, Pinochet spoke defiantly to the nation. Dismissing opposition leaders as "agents of violence," Pinochet claimed to be ruling with the absolute majority support of the Chilean people.

funds even as Spanish authorities seeking his extradition obtained a court order that his assets be frozen. After his return to Chile, Riggs officials arranged for $1.9 million in cashier's checks to be secretly couriered from the United States. At the same time as the Chilean courts declared him mentally incompetent to stand trial on human rights crimes, Pinochet was repeatedly conferring with Riggs officials on the surreptitious transfer of his monies, and personally cashing some thirty-eight checks—each one for the sum of $50,000—at different banks in Santiago.

Revelations of Pinochet's unexplained and hidden wealth, known in Chile as the "Pinocheques" scandal, cost Pinochet his legacy even among those who had benefited from his regime. His supporters in the military, the right-wing media, and the Chilean economic elite, all who had backed the general against accusations of murder, disappearance, torture and terrorism, now abandoned him. The Chilean government initiated no less than three official criminal investigations—to identify the source of Pinochet's illicit funds, as well as to determine whether he was guilty of tax evasion.

Peter Kornbluh, "Pinochet, Augusto," Encyclopedia of Genocide and Crimes Against Humanity, *vol. 2. Detroit: Macmillan Reference USA, 2005, pp. 805–809. Copyright © 2005 Cengage Learning.*

Not until 1988 did Pinochet put his rule to any democratic test, and even then he did so reluctantly. He had promised years earlier to let the Chilean people decide in a plebiscite whether he should continue as president or resign and allow free elections, but as the date approached, Elliott Abrams and other U.S. officials noticed that Pinochet was having second thoughts.

"At the end, he got cold feet," Abrams says, adding, "I don't think there would have been a plebiscite were it not for U.S. pressure."

Pinochet lost the plebiscite; 18 months later, he was replaced by an elected president. But Pinochet remained commander-in-chief of the Chilean Armed Forces and then had himself appointed Senator for Life. Those who had suffered under Pinochet's rule could not seek redress for the wrongs committed against them and they continued to dwell on Pinochet's cruelty.

Ariel Dorfman recalls a day when Chilean investigators found the bodies of people who had disappeared during the early days of Pinochet's rule. They were buried, two to a coffin, in one of Chile's general cemeteries.

"These were men who had been disappeared from their families for 15, 16 years, and Pinochet said, 'Whoever put them two to a coffin should be congratulated because he saved the Chilean government the price of more nails.'" Dorfman says.

While Dorfman and others continued to demand that Pinochet be held accountable for the crimes committed under his direction; Fernando Alessandri and other Chileans argued that Pinochet should be appreciated, not punished.

"The Pinochet regime has many mistakes, very serious mistakes, but these are mistakes that should always be kept in perspective," Alessandri says. "His biggest legacy will be that he opened the country's economy to the world and brought the world to the country."

Pinochet did finally face judgment, but it took a foreign government to get the process started. A Spanish judge who had been investigating crimes against Spanish citizens in Chile ordered Pinochet arrested on charges of genocide and terrorism. He was served with the warrant while staying at a medical clinic in London.

Suddenly, Pinochet—hero to some, villain to others—became yet another thing: a test case in international law.

Ariel Dorfman, now a novelist and a playwright, is pleased.

"He . . . will forever be remembered as the man who inaugurated a new leap in the concept of human rights, which is: Heads of states do not have impunity for those things they have done in crimes against humanity. Humanity can judge them for what they did against us all," Dorfman says.

In the end, the British government concluded that Pinochet was medically unfit to stand trial and allowed him to return to Chile. But he had lost his swagger. Shortly after his return, a Chilean court stripped Pinochet of the immunity he'd enjoyed as a member of the Chilean Senate.

A Chilean investigative judge indicted him for his role in the kidnapping and execution of political prisoners in 1973. It was only his poor medical condition that allowed Pinochet to avoid a trial in his native land.

VIEWPOINT 3

The United Nations Drafts a Resolution on Human Rights Violations in Chile

United Nations

The following viewpoint is the entire text of the United Nation's first resolution on the protection of human rights in Chile. Released in late 1974, it represents the first time that the UN General Assembly acknowledged the grave humanitarian crisis in Chile, making clear how quickly the international community took notice of alleged atrocities. Similar resolutions then followed each year until Augusto Pinochet voluntarily returned Chile to functional democracy in 1990. Although the United Nations regularly expressed dismay at conditions in Chile, no direct action was taken to "restore and safeguard basic human rights in Chile."

The General Assembly,

Convinced of its responsibility under the Charter of the United Nations to promote and encourage respect for human rights and fundamental freedoms for all,

Recalling that, in accordance with the Universal Declaration of Human Rights, everyone has the right to life, liberty and security

United Nations, "Protection of Human Rights in Chile," United Nations Documentation Library, November 6, 1974.

of person and the right not to be subjected to arbitrary arrest, detention or exile or to torture or cruel, inhuman or degrading treatment or punishment,

Recalling also its resolution 3059 (XXVIII) of 2 November 1973 [a UN resolution rejecting "any form of torture and other cruel, inhuman, or degrading treatment or punishment"],

Taking into account the deep concern expressed by the Commission on Human Rights about reports from a wide variety of sources relating to gross and massive violations of human rights in Chile, particularly those involving a threat to human life and liberty,

Taking note of the appeal made by the Economic and Social Council, in its resolution 1873 (LVI) of 17 May 1974, to the Chilean authorities to take all necessary steps to restore and safeguard basic human rights and fundamental freedoms in that country, particularly in those cases involving a threat to human life and liberty,

Noting that the Sub-Commission on Prevention of Discrimination and Protection of Minorities, in its resolution 8 (XXVII) of 21 August 1974, made an urgent appeal to the Chilean authorities to respect the Universal Declaration of Human Rights and to comply with the International Covenants on Human Rights signed and ratified by the Government of Chile,

Noting also that the International Labour Conference, in its resolution X of 24 June 1974, urged the Chilean authorities, *inter alia,* [a legal phrase meaning "among other things"] to cease violations of human rights and trade union rights, to guarantee the life and freedom of arrested, deported or imprisoned workers, militant workers and trade union leaders and members of any political party, to put an end to the practice of torture, to close down the concentration camps and to abolish the special tribunals, and decided to urge the speedy expedition to Chile of the Fact-Finding and Conciliation Commission on Freedom of Association as well as the setting up of a commission of inquiry,

Considering that, notwithstanding all the appeals made by various organs of the United Nations system, gross and massive violations of human rights, such as arbitrary arrest, torture and cruel, inhuman and degrading treatment of political prisoners and detainees, including former members of the Chilean Government and Parliament, continue to be reported,

1. *Expresses its deepest concern* that constant flagrant violations of basic human rights and fundamental freedoms in Chile continue to be reported;
2. *Reiterates* its repudiation of all forms of torture and other cruel, inhuman or degrading treatment or punishment;
3. *Urges* the Chilean authorities to respect fully the principles of the Universal Declaration of Human Rights and to take all necessary steps to restore and safeguard basic human rights and fundamental freedoms, particularly those involving a threat to human life and liberty, to release all persons who have been detained without charge or imprisoned solely for political reasons and to continue to grant safe conduct to those who desire it;
4. *Endorses* the recommendation made by the Sub-Commission on Prevention of Discrimination and Protection of Minorities, in its resolution 8 (XXVII), that the Commission on Human Rights at its thirty-first session should study the reported violations of human rights in Chile, with particular reference to torture and cruel, inhuman or degrading treatment or punishment;
5. *Requests* the President of the twenty-ninth session of the General Assembly and the Secretary-General to assist in any way they may deem appropriate in the re-

establishment of basic human rights and fundamental freedoms in Chile in the light of paragraph 3 above;

6. *Requests* the Secretary-General to submit a report to the General Assembly at its thirtieth session on the action taken and progress achieved under paragraphs 3 to 5 above.

Viewpoint 4

A Sampling of Documented Cases of Torture in Chile

Amnesty International

In the spring of 1982 a delegation of doctors and representatives from Amnesty International visited Chile to investigate and document victims' claims of torture by Chilean authorities between March 1980 and April 1982. The following viewpoints come from the delegation's report that generally corroborated the victims' stories. Their accounts also implicate Chilean doctors who often assisted in state-sponsored torture, both as direct participants and by giving medical examinations before and after interrogations. Amnesty International is a global organization dedicated to protecting and expanding human rights throughout the world.

Case No. 1: Pedro Leonardo López Fabbri

Personal Details He is 28 and worked as a school teacher until his imprisonment in 1975. Since then he has been a clothing retailer. He was married in 1974 and has two sons, aged three and six.

State of Health Before Arrest At the age of six, he sustained a trauma to the head and lost consciousness. An electro-

Amnesty International, *Chile: Evidence of Torture: An Amnesty International Report*. London, UK: Amnesty International Publications, 1983, pp. 29–47.

encephalogram test was taken and found to be normal. He has noticed some weakening of the muscles of the left hand, which is especially apparent under conditions of stress. No medical examination has ever revealed any neurological abnormalities.

Previous Detention and Alleged Torture He was arrested on 11 September 1973 [during the military coup] in Valparaíso and held until 16 September. While in detention he was struck behind his right ear with a rifle butt. He did not lose consciousness. He was also struck on his left knee and left elbow. He was not systematically tortured.

From 6 April until 27 June 1975 he was detained in Silva Palma navy detention centre in Valparaíso. For the first 22 days he was held incommunicado, during which time he claims to have undergone psychological torture involving threats and accusations broadcast to him and the other prisoners for about eight hours a day. During this period of detention he tried to commit suicide by throwing himself out of a second-storey window but was prevented from doing so.

Time and Place of Arrest and Detention He was arrested again on 25 March 1982. He was taken to the CNI [Central Nacional de Informaciones, the Chilean secret police] centre in Santiago where he was held until 4 April when he was transferred to Valparaíso, from where he was released on 8 April.

Duration of Alleged Torture He said he was tortured at the CNI centre on seven days; on the last five days the torture was exclusively psychological.

Interrogation and Torture *His account of events was as follows:* He was arrested at 2.30 P.M. on 25 March 1982. No arrest-warrant was shown. He was blindfolded and forced into a car, in which he was driven for about half an hour. When they reached their destination he was led down a concrete spiral staircase to a large room where he was told to undress and then was given overalls and zapatillas (lightweight footwear). His blindfold was exchanged for a mask. He was then taken to his cell, which measured about 1.5m by 2m and a little over 2m high. The cell contained a concrete bunk plus mattress, pillow and a blanket.

His first interrogation took place two days after arrest. It was conducted in another room in the presence of about five other people. He was asked about his connections with political parties. He was beaten: struck on the head, punched on the right side of his chest and beaten with a rubber truncheon on the shoulders. Afterwards he was stretched out on a bed, to which his wrists were tied with cloth, this causing sharp, painful extension of the elbows. A cloth strap was tied round his thighs; his ankles were tied down and his head was put in a special device which prevented him from raising it. He was gagged with a towel. A metal object was fastened to the inner side of his right foot. Two electrodes (in addition to the one fastened to his foot) were then used to administer electric shocks to the lobe of his right ear, to his chest, abdomen, testicles, penis area, anus, legs and the soles of his feet. He was electrically tortured three times that day. He thought the electrodes used were electric wires. While he was being electrically tortured he could hear a generator, so he believed it was possible to vary the current. He did not lose consciousness during the electric torture, nor did he have generalized convulsions.

Two days later he was again interrogated and electrically tortured while naked.

Other types of torture inflicted on him included burning with a cigarette lighter in the kidney region and on the palms of both hands. The burns were superficial and left no marks.

He was in addition psychologically tortured for five days, on two of which he was interrogated for eight hours. During these sessions his family's and his own life were threatened and an attempt was made to hypnotize him by a man nicknamed "Doc", who was large and very fat. His mask was removed. He was first told to breathe deeply, then that the pain in his head was being shifted down to his legs. He was then told to conduct an imaginary orchestra and behave as though he were watching a Chaplin film. He was not actually hypnotized but behaved as though he were. He was also asked to write his life story.

He was held incommunicado for 10 days at the CNI centre, masked throughout, except when he was in his cell. He wore overalls and *zapatillas.* The food was good. He was allowed to use the toilet, but his cell was cold and he could not get warm, even though he had a blanket. His cell light was always on.

Medical Examination and/or Attention During Detention Immediately after he arrived at the CNI centre he had a medical examination, carried out, he believed, by a doctor. It consisted of examination of the heart and lungs and measurement of blood pressure. He was asked whether he had any bruises or other marks on his body and what illnesses he had previously had. The doctor was assisted by a woman—a nurse, he presumed. When he showed symptoms of anxiety, the doctor gave him two tranquillizers. He could not see the doctor because of the mask, but thought he was about 50. The doctor made a record of his findings, which the subject later saw when he signed his release papers. He was examined in a special room.

While in prison he had diarrhoea. A medical assistant took him to the doctor, who provided treatment and recommended that he be allowed to stay in bed all day—which was normally forbidden.

Before he was transferred from the CNI centre to Valparaiso he was medically examined again.

Early Symptoms Described During one of the torture sessions he had difficulty breathing and was given manual artificial respiration.

He said he had pain, swelling and an accumulation of blood around the elbow which he ascribed to the stretching of his elbows during electric torture. He had pain, swelling, discolouration, weakness and enhanced sensitivity to touch in his legs and feet. There were sharp pains and swelling in the part of his thorax where he had been punched on the right side. He had observed skin changes where he had been electrically tortured: the lowest part of the abdomen, both inguinal regions [upper groin and thigh], the front of his thighs and the insides of his legs at the crura [lower leg]. He explained that the lesions were small and round with brown scabs. After about a week these scabs dropped off leaving some lighter areas which later became hyper-pigmented.

During torture he suffered from tachycardia [elevated heart rate].

He lost 2kg while in prison. Once he vomited, and he had diarrhoea, with accompanying abdominal pains, for four days. There was no blood in the stools.

For four days he had blood in his urine and had pain when he urinated; his testicles were swollen.

While in detention he had headaches around the forehead.

He also suffered from insomnia and nightmares. He was depressed, felt passive and lethargic and easily got tired. He would weep for almost no reason.

Present Symptoms Described The leg is still painful after walking for only a short while. There is also some swelling, and he feels weaker and more sensitive to touch. He complains of pains on the inner side of the right elbow. There are no gastrointestinal or urological symptoms. He still has headaches around the forehead, particularly when he is under stress.

He feels isolated, somewhat as if he were "under a glass bell", but does not have any actual relationship problems.

He suffers from insomnia and nightmares and he awakens easily and frequently. He has been given tranquillizers, which he says help. He feels rather depressed, somewhat passive and lethargic and gets tired easily. He is emotionally labile [unstable].

Medical Documentation There is a certificate of a physical examination by a local doctor, dated 12 April 1982, which states:

Physical examination: There were groups of punctiform, small round burns, scattered over various parts of the body and red burns in the inguinal region and on the thighs, legs and ankles.

He had pain and tenderness in both ankles and in the middle line of the right thigh. Part of the skin on the thigh and feet is whitish-pink with desquamation of the epidermis, as if punched out. The thigh lesion is 10cm long and 0.5cm wide.

Diagnosis: Groups of several small, punctiform burns, clustered and diffused (burns caused by electricity); circular erosions on thighs and scabs on the feet; contusion of the ribs on the right side; anxiety.

Clinical Examination (One Month After the Alleged Torture) He seemed somewhat tense but otherwise normal mentally.

There was tenderness in both temporal regions.

Thorax [chest]: There was local tenderness and pain on springing the ribs. This was most marked over the right eighth and ninth ribs in the mid-clavicular line.

X-ray thorax (27 April 1982): Normal.

There was tenderness in the trapezius muscle of the shoulder.

There was tenderness and slight swelling of the right medial epicondyle [humerus] but no limitation of movement.

There was oedemic swelling [swelling due to accumulated fluid beneath the skin] of both ankles, particularly on the right side. There was marked tenderness over the medial aspect of the lower tibiae [shin], particularly on the right.

Peripheral nervous system: There was altered sensation in the medial part of both legs, especially of the right leg. There was normal sensitivity to pain.

Skin: A number of small, hyperpigmented [dark] spots, about 2mm in diameter and often present in clusters, were evident on the entire abdomen as well as proximally on the thighs

Usual Interrogation Methods Under Pinochet

Certain methods were routinely practiced on all prisoners held at secret facilities. These sites had permanent installations for applying such methods and personnel trained to use them. . . .

Such methods were:

- The "grill," that is, applying electrical current to prisoners while they were tied to a metal bed spring. The current was applied to the most sensitive parts of the body.
- Suspension, that is, hanging the victim either by the wrists or by the wrists and knees for long periods of time. Sometimes the guards made it worse by hanging onto the victim themselves thus adding their weight. While thus suspended the person was given electric shocks, and was beaten, cut, or humiliated.
- Immersion, or the "submarine," which consisted of pushing a person's head into a vessel of liquid, generally filthy water, and holding it there to the point of asphyxiation, and doing so over and over. One variation of this method was the so-called "dry submarine," in which a plastic bag was used to cut off a person's air supply.
- Beatings of all kinds, inflicted with fists, feet, rifle butts, and chains on different parts of the body, causing serious wounds and even killing people. Hitting people over the ears

adjacent to the perineum [crotch]. On the right leg were two scars measuring 17mm by 7mm and 9mm by 5mm. The central parts of the scars were pale, atrophic and shiny, and there was a reddish-purple poorly defined margin.

Conclusion The medical delegates found consistency between the torture alleged and the symptoms described. There was consistency also between the symptoms described and the descrip-

> with cupped hands, or the "telephone," left some people with permanently impaired hearing. . . .
>
> Other methods were also often used, but they were generally extraordinary measures taken when other methods were not producing results. The official in charge of the interrogation made the decision to use such methods. They included:
>
> - Torture of a psychological nature, that is, abducting a relative of the prisoner who was not politically involved and torturing or sexually abusing that person in the presence of the one being interrogated, or perhaps threatening such possibilities.
> - Wounds caused by bullets, cuts, or even once breaking a person's legs by running over them in a vehicle, as well as other fractures.
> - Rape or other sexual assaults or the threat of them. It seems that at some places such practices were regarded as an excess and were the work of guards or lower ranking personnel without the permission of their superiors. At other sites, however, as is noted, it was common practice.
>
> Apparently on some rare occasions officers used extreme methods, because they became carried away with anger or sadism. Among these were burning prisoner's bodies with boiling liquids and unnatural acts involving animals.
>
> Report of the Chilean National Commission on Truth and Reconciliation. *Notre Dame, Indiana: University of Notre Dame Press, 1993.*

tion given by a local doctor two weeks after the alleged torture. The findings of the examination by the medical delegates, carried out one month after the alleged torture, were consistent with the symptoms described.

Case No. 2: Anonymous

Personal Details He is 21, unmarried and lives with his parents. He went through high school and is now doing a course in journalism. While he was a student he was also for a time a telephone operator but was dismissed before being detained. He is supported by his parents.

State of Health Before Arrest When he was two he had tonsillitis, which was apparently complicated by endocarditis [inflammation of the heart]. Prophylactic [preventative] penicillin was prescribed during the subsequent 10 winters.

Time and Place of Arrest and Detention He was arrested in the first quarter of 1982. He was held at the CNI centre in Santiago for 19 days then transferred to the *Cárcel Publica* (Public Prison), where he stayed until his release on bail, 45 days after arrest.

Duration of Alleged Torture He said he was tortured on 19 days. On the last 14 the torture was exclusively psychological.

Interrogation and Torture *His account of events was as follows:* About 12 people in civilian clothes broke into his home in the first quarter of 1982. No arrest-warrant was shown. They searched the premises for two hours and arrested him, his father and another relative. They hooded and handcuffed him, then drove him to the CNI centre.

For the first five days he was interrogated several times a day, and simultaneously tortured, mainly physically. He was slapped and struck on the head, mouth, body and genitals, and his buttocks and extremities were kicked. He was also electrically tortured on two occasions, each lasting five minutes. He was made to sit on a chair and electric current was applied to his back via a cable conducting current from a machine he thought was hand-driven.

The interrogations continued for the next 14 days he spent at the CNI centre. They included threats, including threats of execution (a pistol was aimed at his temple) and threats to arrest his family.

He often heard his father and relative screaming while they were being tortured. And he heard the voice of a woman who was not his mother, although he was told it was her voice so frequently that eventually he believed it was. (She has not been imprisoned.)

He was held incommunicado throughout the 19 days in a 2m by 2m concrete cell containing a concrete bunk plus a thin mattress. He wore overalls and *zapatillas* and was forced to wear a mask except when alone in his cell. His cell light was always on.

Medical Examination and/or Attention During Detention Both before he was tortured at the CNI centre and before he left he was given a superficial medical examination, by a doctor, he thought. It included measurement of blood pressure and auscultation of [listening to] the chest.

His pulse was taken every day he was at the CNI centre. On one occasion he was given tablets for diarrhoea.

Early Symptoms Described He had aches and pains and felt weak all over, especially in his arms and legs.

After being hit on the mouth he lost an upper tooth, No. 24, and the frenulum [connective tissue between lip and gums] of his lower lip bled.

He had diarrhoea for three or four days while at the CNI centre. He had pain in the buttocks and near the anus (as a result of kickings, he said). His left testicle too was painful (because of the beatings, he thought).

Throughout his detention he had headaches every day. After being allowed to remove the mask he found his vision was impaired. Periodically he had double vision and his eyes got tired when he read (the letters began to blur after about 10 minutes).

He got retrosternal pain [chest pain] several times a week, and palpitations of the heart lasting for about 15 minutes, when resting. (This was related to anxiety, he thought.) He had never had such symptoms before. While he was at the CNI centre he lost his

The old Valparaíso prison, where many political prisoners were detained and tortured under the Pinochet regime, was closed down in 1999. © Paolo Messina/Alamy.

sense of time—could not tell night from day. He felt suicidal because of anxiety lest he reveal information. He suffered from insomnia and nightmares and was gloomy, emotionally labile and indifferent.

Present Symptoms Described He feels unusually tired and weak and still has pain in his left testicle, although this is diminishing. He gets headaches starting at about noon every day. They are exacerbated by reading, and he still has vision problems: periodic double vision and blurring of letters on the page after he has been reading for about 10 minutes.

He still feels gloomy, emotionally labile and indifferent. He stays at home most of the time and is not involved in anything (partly because he is under surveillance and cannot meet his former friends outside his home).

He suffers from continuing, though less frequent, episodes of precordial pain and palpitations of the heart while resting (probably due to anxiety), and from serious insomnia and nightmares.

Clinical Examination He seemed depressed. Although prepared to cooperate, he was passive, slow and hard to make contact with. He had difficulty expressing himself.

The clinical examination revealed bad teeth, many of them decayed. There was a large cavity in No. 24 and the crown was almost completely gone. The lower frenulum of the lip was irregular and had small sores on it. He had muscular pains in the left flank and tenderness in the epididymis.

Conclusion The medical delegates found consistency between the torture alleged, the symptoms described and the results of the physical examination. . . .

Case No. 4: Anonymous

Personal Details She is 19. Before her arrest she was training to be a social worker. Since her release she has been unemployed. She is unmarried. The man she lived with before her arrest is now in prison and she lives with her uncle.

State of Health Before Arrest She was in good health.

Time and Place of Arrest and Detention She was arrested in Santiago in the first quarter of 1981. No arrest-warrant was shown. She was taken to the CNI centre in the city and held there until her release 19 days later.

Duration of Alleged Torture She claimed that while she was at the CNI centre she was tortured on 17 days, on the last three of which the torture was exclusively psychological.

Interrogation and Torture *Her account of events was as follows:* during interrogation she was slapped all over the body and punched in the face, breasts and abdomen. She was kicked on the buttocks and backs of the thighs, usually while lying down. On one occasion when she was in her cell an interrogator seized her hair and banged the back and right side of her head against the wall. She did not lose consciousness. She was electrically tortured. She was stretched out on a metal bed with hands and feet bound. She was given shocks on the temples, chest and heel. A metal object was applied to her vaginal labia [lip] and she was electrically tortured there, but the device was not forced inside.

On about the eighth day she was sexually tortured. She was stripped naked and her blindfold was removed. She was made to lie on the floor then kicked and raped by four men, one of whom subjected her to fellatio [oral sex performed on a male]. This type of torture lasted about an hour. They also threatened to violate her with a dog and to lock her in a room with rats.

She was told the man she had been living with had been killed. She was then taken into a room where a corpse lay with its face covered and told it was this man. She knew it was not however, as the body's height and build were different from his. The corpse had been split open down the middle and there were wounds on the abdomen. It was beginning to decompose, and she was forced to lie right by it facing it. At one stage the towel was removed from its decomposing face.

On five occasions she was taken into a small, very hot room and left there for a few minutes. She had a burning feeling all over but did not think she actually was burned.

She was taken into a room full of rats, but managed to jump up on a bed and so escaped from them. She was threatened: the interrogators said they would kill her, the man she had been living with and her parents. She was also insulted and called a whore.

On each of the last five days of her imprisonment a "friendly" interrogator visited her. He was very fatherly and asked her about her friendships and her life history. He repeatedly assured her (almost hypnotizing her in the process) that she had been very well treated.

She was partially deprived of sleep for the first 14 days, getting only a few hours' sleep between each interrogation session.

She was held incommunicado throughout her 19 days at the CNI centre. She was blindfold all the time except when in her cell, when being sexually tortured and when confronted with the corpse. She was naked during several of the torture sessions; the rest the time she wore overalls and *zapatillas*.

She was handcuffed all the time (including when she ate) except when she went to the toilet. The food was adequate. The day after her arrival at the CNI centre, she was photographed in her cell, which was about 3m by 2m and contained a concrete bunk, blankets and a pillow.

Medical Examination and/or Attention During Detention On arrival at the CNI centre she was examined by a man, probably, she thought, a doctor. The examination included taking her pulse and blood pressure. She was examined again before release.

After every torture session she was medically examined and her pulse and blood pressure were taken.

The "friendly" interrogator arranged for a doctor to examine her. The doctor said she had caught cold, said she should have more blankets and gave her some tablets.

Medical Personnel Involved in Torture Before she was sexually tortured she was injected with an unknown substance in the right cubital fossa [inner elbow]. (She could not tell who gave her the injection.) She was also injected in the right shoulder.

Early Symptoms Described Her recollection of the first 14 days at the CNI centre was hazy as she had partially lost her sense of time. All she wanted to do was die, and she asked them to kill her rather than keep torturing her. She tried to commit suicide. She fainted several times while being tortured, then recovered consciousness in her cell. She had pains all over her body after being beaten and electrically tortured. She had headaches and vomited (she said there was blood in the vomit). After torture she could not walk very well and her arms, legs and hands were swollen. This condition lasted for about a month. The skin on her right buttock and the outside of her thigh was discoloured but the discolouration faded quite fast. Apart from that she had no marks on her body.

After her release she lost her appetite and her upper abdomen ached after eating; and for some time after release she fell as though she were sleep-walking. She could not weep even though she was miserable. She felt utterly indifferent to everything and wanted to be left alone. She was bothered by noise and light, which gave her a headache. She often lay awake at night; at other times she had nightmares.

She lost 13kg while in detention. (After release she went to a doctor because she was aching all over, especially her back and left knee, and because of a vaginal discharge and irritation. She was treated for a pelvic inflammation disease and urinary tract infection.)

She did not menstruate for the first three months after release and since then has done so somewhat irregularly, her periods being heavier and much more painful than before. Since her release, she has had headaches, especially at the back of the head and around the temples. She went to an optician who told her she needed spectacles. Probably, however, this visual defect is not of recent origin.

For a short time after release she had respiratory difficulties: she coughed and expectorated [coughed up phlegm] and had spells of whistling and gasping when trying to breathe.

Towards the end of her time at the CNI centre she could no longer recall what had happened to her and was not sure whether she had been hypnotized. This loss of memory persisted even after she had been released. She wanted to be alone. Her sleep was disturbed by nightmares; she was afraid and had difficulty falling asleep. Later she went to a psychiatrist and had group therapy. In mid-1981 she broke down during a session with her psychiatrist; then she began to remember what had happened to her at the CNI centre. She had a traumatic experience and spent 15 days in a psychiatric hospital. Gradually she began to remember everything that had occurred at the CNI centre.

After leaving hospital she was in a rehabilitation centre for a week, then visited her parents. On several occasions she has behaved as though she were being tortured—has cried, screamed and flung herself about. This last occurred early in 1982. She has been treated with medication.

Present Symptoms Described Her left knee and back (around the spinal column) still ache when she moves them. She can now breathe normally again and a recent chest X-ray revealed nothing abnormal.

Recently she has had several bouts of vomiting and a heavy feeling in the stomach and acid reflux after eating. It still occasionally hurts when she urinates; however, her doctor has not found any bacteria in her urine.

Her menstrual cycle is somewhat irregular and her periods are heavier than before. She gets menstrual pain during the first three days of each period.

She gets headaches at the back of the head and around the temples. They last about two hours and are bad enough to make her lie down. She has difficulty reading and can do so only for about half an hour at a time without getting a headache. She cannot concentrate for long stretches, and is apt to get restless and feel cooped up. She feels different from how she was before she was arrested and likes to be left on her own.

She suffers from insomnia and awakens easily. She feels more withdrawn and nervous. She still sees a psychiatrist, who has treated her with chlorpromazine [an antipsychotic], imipramine [an anti-depressant] and sleeping tablets.

Clinical Examination (Nearly 14 Months After the Alleged Torture) She seemed somewhat tense and melancholy but was cooperative. In the abdominal region there was tenderness in the upper epigastrium and in both iliac fossae [outer pelvis]. (A gynaecological examination was not carried out.) There was tenderness over the spinal process of thoracic [torso] vertebrae II, III, VIII, IX and X.

Conclusion She said her memory was impaired for about four months and she could not remember certain things she has now said happened to her at the CNI centre.

There are several plausible psychiatric explanations for this. She may be suffering from a reactive psychosis, as is suggested by her loss of time sense, low state of mind plus suicidal thoughts and the fact that she has clearly experienced sufficient emotional trauma to justify such a diagnosis. Or she may have been the victim of a form of hypnotic suggestion, leading her to "forget" what the authorities had done to her and to accept their views totally. Or else her condition may constitute a type of defence mechanism involving a denial of what she went through. Most likely, however, it is a combination of all three.

The medical delegates found complete consistency between the torture alleged and the symptoms described. The findings of their examination, carried out nearly 14 months after the alleged torture, were consistent also with the symptoms described. . . .

Case No. 9: Anonymous

Personal Details He is 28. His father was an officer who resigned after the military coup. He studied history and geography at university, but has not been able to get work as a teacher since graduating in 1979. He therefore became a sales agent. Because of a knee operation, he has been off sick since early 1982. He is married. His wife was pregnant at the time of his arrest. Their child was born 11 days later.

State of Health Before Arrest His left knee was injured in mid-1973 and he was in hospital for almost a month. After he left hospital he continued to suffer pain in the knee, so his left medial meniscus was removed in early 1982.

Ever since 1973 he has had sporadic "nervous heart" attacks with precordial [chest] pain and difficulty in breathing. Apart from this he did not connect any symptoms with his arrest and detention in 1973.

Previous Detention and Alleged Torture He was arrested and held briefly in 1973 after attending a student meeting which was surrounded by the police. He was kicked and pistol-whipped all over. Afterwards, he was taken to a boat called the "Maipo", where he was not actually ill-treated, although he was held in appalling sanitary conditions.

Time and Place of Arrest and Detention He was arrested in the first quarter of 1982 and held at the CNI centre in Valparaíso for 10 days. He was then transferred to the CNI centre in Santiago, where he was held for a week. Then he was moved to Valparaíso prison, where he remained until his unconditional release 21 days after arrest.

Duration of Alleged Torture He was tortured on 10 days; on four of them the torture was exclusively psychological. He was held incommunicado for 16 days.

Interrogation and Torture *His account of events was as follows:* In mid-March five men in plain-clothes who said they were members of SICAR, the *Carabineros*' intelligence agency, searched his home and removed several of his belongings. No arrest-warrant was shown. He was taken down to a car, hooded and threatened.

They drove him to an old house in Valparaíso, where he was made to sit on a chair to which his hands and feet were tied. He was asked about his personal relationships and kept tied to the chair all night.

He stayed tied to the chair throughout the following day, forced to listen to a cassette recording of a Mexican song played over and over again at full volume. The door was opened loudly a number of times during the day, but those who opened it said nothing to him.

That night he was allowed to go to bed but was tied to it by one hand. During the night he was woken up several times by somebody kicking him in the stomach.

Next day he was tied to the chair again and made to listen to music all day. In the evening, he was interrogated and kicked and beaten, mainly in the abdomen and on the back. He was undressed and electrically tortured for about an hour, primarily on the back and neck.

He sat on the chair throughout the next day, listening to the cassette player. In the evening he was interrogated for an hour and a half. During the interrogation he was punched on the body and neck, hit on the back of the head three or four times, slapped on the face and underwent *teléfono* [double ear slaps] from five to 10 times. He was also frequently threatened with "disappearance" and execution.

The next day he was tied to the chair again and made to listen to a loud radio all day. A basic medical examination was carried out by a person who claimed to be a doctor.

He was interrogated for most of the following afternoon. Every time he refused to answer he was punched, mainly on the nose, which bled.

The next day he was interrogated, threatened and insulted, but the day after he was not interrogated—although he was made to spend the entire time sitting tied to a chair.

On the following day a "friendly" interrogator chatted to him all day trying to persuade him to tell the truth and so avoid further torture. Later someone else threatened him again with execution.

He was not interrogated the following day, but the day after his clothes were returned to him and he was made to sign various forms. Then some evidently important person came and shouted that they were incorrectly filled in. All his belongings were again removed and he was taken down to a car. He thought he was going to be killed and felt both frightened and resigned. Instead, however, he was taken to the CNI centre in Santiago where he was given overalls and *zapatillas* and was blindfolded. He was put in a small concrete cell measuring about 2m by 1.5m. That evening a person he took to be a doctor examined him with a stethoscope and measured his blood pressure, and he was interrogated yet again, this interrogation being far worse than any of the previous ones. He was made to lie on a bed and was severely beaten, including on the knee which had just been operated on. He was electrically tortured more severely than before with two electrodes, one attached to his chest, the other shifted about from his testicles to his right ankle to the lobe of his right ear. Later the *picana* [high-voltage, low-current electrical] torture was inflicted with a pencil-shaped object on his face and lips. A dry cloth was put over his mouth and nose a number of times, which made him feel as though he were being suffocated. Each time he nearly fainted. When he was finally taken back to his cell he heard the voice and screams of a friend (also interviewed by the medical delegates—Case No. 1).

He was left in his cell throughout the next two days. Someone who he thought may have been a doctor applied cream to his bruises.

The following day he was interrogated and beaten, in particular on the abdomen and back.

Next day the "doctor" came to his cell and tried to hypnotize him, but, by making a strenuous effort, he managed to resist this.

He was taken to the *Fiscalía Militar* (Military Prosecutor's Office) the following day and, still blindfolded, made to sign some papers.

Next day he was given back his clothes and belongings and driven to the CNI centre in Valparaíso then on to Valparaíso prison, where he was no longer kept in isolation.

He was freed after 21 days but followed by agents for two days after release.

Résumé of Interrogation and Torture He was slapped, particularly in the face. He underwent *teléfono* a number of times. He was frequently punched, once on the neck, once on the nose (which gave him a nosebleed) and many times in the abdomen and on the back, arms and legs. He was frequently kicked, in particular on the buttocks and the knee that had just been operated on.

He was electrically tortured twice: once in Valparaíso for an hour and once in Santiago. The shocks were administered on the lobe of his right ear, chest, testicles, right ankle, neck and back. *Picana* torture (at a lower voltage) was inflicted too, particularly on the lips, earlobes and cheeks.

He was gagged a number of times in such a way that he could not breathe and nearly fainted.

He was partially deprived of sleep the first two nights and made to spend an entire night naked, as well as being naked during several interrogation sessions.

He received many threats. He was threatened with execution and "disappearance", with being tortured in other ways, and with the imprisonment of his wife. He was tortured by noise for many days: forced to hear the same tune on a cassette player again and again at maximum volume.

An attempt was made to hypnotize him, and the "friendly" interrogator tried to get him to give information.

He was kept in isolation and blindfolded for 16 days. For the first 10 days he was forced to sit up straight, tied to a chair. Except for the first night, when he was forced to remain sitting, he was allowed to sleep in bed. For his five days in Santiago he was kept in a concrete cell measuring about 1.5m by 2m.

Medical Examination and/or Attention During Detention Once in Valparaíso and the first day in Santiago he was examined by someone claiming to be a doctor. During his final days at the CNI centre in Santiago he was given ointment to rub on his skin in order, he thought, to hasten the disappearance of his bruises.

Early Symptoms Described After being tortured he was tired and stiff, felt sore all over and could hardly move. Near both elbows were two parallel blue stripes which he said were the result of the tight binding of his arms with cord during torture. The cords were tied especially tightly during electric torture when his arms moved involuntarily. There were bruises on the right hypogastrium [lower stomach], as well as medially on the left leg just under the knee. His nose bled after being punched, his lip was swollen for a week and his ears itched and were scaly in the auditory canal. He suffered from precordial pain in the chest, without radiation, and had difficulty breathing for about half an hour several times a week. This happened particularly at night, and he himself believed it was due to anxiety since he had had similar anxiety attacks before being arrested. He had nightmares and his memory was somewhat impaired. Just after he was released he found himself forgetting small matters, such as where he had put things, appointments and telephone numbers. He was emotionally labile, irritable and aggressive.

Present Symptoms Described He still has slight discomfort in his left knee and pain in the medial part of his left calf, where he can feel a hard lump near the tibia. He suffers from "nervous" attacks of difficulty in breathing about once a week. His memory is slightly impaired.

Clinical Examination (One Month After the Alleged Torture) He was well-balanced and relaxed, cooperated with the interviewer and was able to give a clear and detailed account of what had happened to him.

There was some soreness in the medial anterior cleft of his left knee, and a slight atrophy of the quadriceps [thigh] muscle. On "the medial side of the left tibia, between 16cm and 19cm below the knee, there was a 3cm by 2cm hard, indolent [nonpartial] lump, unattached to the skin and tibia (it felt very much like an organized haematoma [encapsulated blood clot]). The skin over the knot was unchanged. Medial to this area and between 12cm and 16cm distal to the knee joint a 5cm-long, 1cm-diameter, rod-shaped indolent swelling could be felt (probably an area of superficial phlebitis [inflamed veins]).

Near both elbows were two sets of two light brown pigmented parallel stripes 1cm wide and separated by 2cm, crossing each other approximately in the middle of the bend of the elbow.

Conclusion The medical delegates found consistency between the torture alleged, the symptoms described and the clinical findings.

Viewpoint 5

The CIA Explains Its Actions in Chile

Central Intelligence Agency

In response to a 2000 amendment to the Intelligence Authorization Act, the Central Intelligence Agency (CIA) was required to explain the depth of US involvement in the overthrow of Salvador Allende's government in Chile. When Representative Maurice Hinchey sponsored the amendment, he explained, "This very sordid chapter in American history needs to be held up to the bright light so that everyone can see what went on under orders from the president of the United States, the secretary of state, and the attorney general." The following viewpoint, also known as the "Hinchey Report," discusses the CIA's activities to undermine Allende's government, support Pinochet's coup, and allow crimes against humanity to continue in Chile. In the report the CIA repeatedly admits to direct knowledge of government-sponsored torture as early as 1974.

Many of Pinochet's officers were involved in systematic and widespread human rights abuses following Allende's ouster. Some of these were contacts or agents of the CIA or US military. The IC [intelligence community within the US government] followed then-current guidance for reporting such abuses and admonished its Chilean agents against such

Central Intelligence Agency, "CIA Activities in Chile," September 18, 2000. www.cia.gov.

behavior. Today's [2000] much stricter reporting standards were not in force and, if they were, we suspect many agents would have been dropped.

In the 1960s and the early 1970s, as part of the US Government policy to try to influence events in Chile, the CIA undertook specific covert action projects in Chile. Those hereby acknowledged are described below. The overwhelming objective—firmly rooted in the policy of the period—was to discredit Marxist-leaning political leaders, especially Dr. Salvador Allende, and to strengthen and encourage their civilian and military opponents to prevent them from assuming power.

At the direction of the White House and interagency policy coordination committees, CIA undertook . . . sustained propaganda efforts, including financial support for major news media, against Allende and other Marxists. Political action projects supported selected parties before and after the 1964 elections and after Allende's 1970 election. . . .

CIA officers were aware of and reported to analysts and policymakers in 1973 that General Pinochet and the forces that overthrew the Allende Government were conducting a severe campaign against leftists and perceived political enemies in the early months after the coup. Activities of some security services portended a long-term effort to suppress opponents. In January 1974, CIA officers and assets were tasked to report on human rights violations by the Chilean government.

The CIA had liaison relationships in Chile with the primary purpose of securing assistance in gathering intelligence on external targets. The CIA offered these services assistance in internal organization and training to combat subversion and terrorism from abroad, not in combating internal opponents of the government. The CIA also used these relationships to admonish these services concerning human rights abuses in Chile. The policy community and CIA recognized that the relationships opened the CIA to possible identification with the liaison services' internal operations involving human rights abuses but determined that the contact was necessary for CIA's mission. . . .

Historical Context of CIA Action in Chile

The historical backdrop sheds important light on the policies, practices, and perceived urgency prevalent at that time. The Cuban revolution and emergence of Communist parties in Latin America had brought the Cold War to the Western Hemisphere. Thousands of Chilean military officers came to the United States for training, which included presentations on the impact of global communism on their own country. After Allende won a plurality in the Presidential election on 4 September 1970, the consensus at the highest levels of the US Government was that an Allende Presidency would seriously hurt US national interests.

Efforts by the United States to support anti-Communist forces in Chile date back to the late 1950s and reflect the rivalry between the United States and the Soviet Union for influence throughout the Third World. The growing strength of the Chilean left, along with continuing fragmentation by conservative and moderate political forces, became increasing concerns through the 1960–70s to the United States, which wanted to avoid the emergence of "another Cuba" in the Western Hemisphere.

According to the Church Committee report, in their meeting with CIA Director Richard Helms and Attorney General John Mitchell on 15 September 1970 President Nixon and his National Security Advisor, Henry Kissinger, directed the CIA to prevent Allende from taking power. They were "not concerned [about the] risks involved," according to Helms' notes. In addition to political action, Nixon and Kissinger, according to Helms's notes, ordered steps to "make the economy scream."

These Cold War attitudes persisted into the Pinochet era. After Pinochet came to power, senior policymakers appeared reluctant to criticize human rights violations, taking to task US diplomats urging greater attention to the problem. US military assistance and sales grew significantly during the years of

Firemen remove victims from the remains of a car bombing in Washington, DC, on September 21, 1976. The former Chilean ambassador to the United States and his American aide were both killed in the blast. © AP Images.

greatest human rights abuses. According to a previously released Memorandum of Conversation, Kissinger in June 1976 indicated to Pinochet that the US Government was sympathetic to his regime, although Kissinger advised some progress on human rights in order to improve Chile's image in the US Congress. . . .

Violations of Human Rights Committed by Officers or Covert Agents and Employees of the CIA

In January 1974 CIA issued a directive to all CIA staff to collect clandestine information on torture in Chile; this message directed CIA staff to work through all available agents and channels of

The Assassination of Orlando Letelier

Marcos Orlando Letelier del Solar was a prominent Socialist politician, diplomat, and economist under President Salvador Allende. Letelier's expertise in the copper industry led Allende to appoint him ambassador to the United States in 1971. (US corporations held major investments in Chilean copper mines until the industry was nationalized in the 1970s.) Two years later Allende called Letelier back to Chile, where the former ambassador served as the minister of foreign affairs and later as minister of the interior.

At the time of the coup Letelier was Chile's minister of defense. He was the first high-ranking official in Allende's government arrested by Augusto Pinochet's military junta. During the next year Letelier was shuffled between prisons and concentration camps throughout Chile and brutally tortured. Bowing to international pressure, Pinochet's government abruptly released Letelier in 1974, on the condition that he leave Chile immediately.

Letelier briefly settled in Caracas, Venezuela (whose mayor had a major role in Letelier's release), before moving to Washington, DC. Letelier joined several research institutes and taught at American University in addition to writing, speaking, and lobbying tirelessly against the Pinochet regime in Chile. These efforts established Letelier as the leading voice of worldwide Chilean resistance.

In 1976, however, Pinochet stripped Letelier of his Chilean citizenship. Just weeks later Letelier died in Washington, DC, in a car bombing that also killed his assistant, Ronni Moffitt, and injured her husband, Michael Moffitt. Later that year Michael Townley, an American citizen, was convicted for his part in the bombing. Townley had connections with the CIA but at the time was working for the Chilean secret police, the *Dirección de Inteligencia Nacional* (DINA). During his trial he testified that Pinochet had personally planned the assassination. These claims were corroborated in 1993 with the trial and conviction of former DINA chief Manuel Contreras, another participant in the plot. Despite these sworn testimonies, Augusto Pinochet was never indicted for the murders of Orlando Letelier or Ronni Moffitt.

influence to induce the Chilean Government to modify repressive measures, particularly to eliminate torture. CIA actively used its contacts, especially with members of services notorious for human rights abuses, to emphasize that human rights abuses were detrimental to the government's credibility within their own country, damaging to their international reputation, and unacceptable to the US Government. In some cases, such contacts enabled the CIA to obtain intelligence on human rights abuses that would not have otherwise been available.

Given the wide variety and nature of CIA contacts in Chile, the issue of human rights was handled in various ways over the years. Some examples:

- Before the 1973 coup, the issue of human rights was not addressed in liaison contacts and intelligence reporting.
- One CIA contact was known to be involved in an abortive coup attempt on 29 June 1973, and another was involved in the successful 11 September 1973 coup.
- In October 1973, the CIA had credible information that a high-level contact was involved in specific human rights abuses; contact was severed.
- Although the CIA had information indicating that a high-level contact was a hard-liner and therefore more likely to commit abuses, contact with him was allowed to continue in the absence of concrete information about human rights abuses.
- CIA maintained indirect contact with a source in close contact with human rights violators. There was no evidence that the source engaged in abuses, but he almost certainly knew about the practice. The intelligence value of the contact was sufficiently important that the contact was not dropped.
- In the case of an individual about whom the CIA had information concerning a corruption issue that may have

been related to human rights issues, a decision was made to seek contact given his position and potential intelligence value.

- In more than one case, in light of the contacts' service affiliation and position, it seemed likely that they were involved in, knew about or covered up human rights abuses. However, because such contacts allowed the CIA to accomplish its intelligence reporting mission and maintain a channel through which to voice concerns about human rights abuses, contact was continued.
- In a few cases, although the CIA had knowledge that the contact represented a service with a known history of human rights abuses, contact was continued because refusing such contact would have had a negative impact on the CIA intelligence collection mission.
- In some cases careful checks of contacts' human rights records were not conducted, and a deliberate risk-versus-gain decision was not made. In such cases, if a contact was deemed to have intelligence value, continuing contact was authorized.
- Information concerning human rights abuses of then current and former CIA contacts was disseminated to the intelligence and policy communities.

The CIA's Relationship with Contreras

During a period between 1974 and 1977, CIA maintained contact with Manuel Contreras Sepulveda, who later became notorious for his involvement in human rights abuses. The US Government policy community approved CIA's contact with Contreras, given his position as chief of the primary intelligence organization in Chile, as necessary to accomplish the CIA's mission, in spite of concerns that this relationship might lay the CIA open to charges of aiding internal political repression. From the start, the CIA made it clear to Contreras was that it would not support any of his activities or activities of his service which might be construed as "internal political repression." In its contacts with Contreras, the CIA urged him to adhere to a 17 January 1974 circular, issued by the Chilean Ministry of Defense, spelling out guidelines for handling prisoners in a manner consistent with the 1949 Geneva Convention.

The relationship, while correct, was not cordial and smooth, particularly as evidence of Contreras' role in human rights abuses emerged. In December 1974, the CIA concluded that Contreras was not going to improve his human rights performance. However, Contreras' assistance in the first quarter of 1975 in gaining the release of some PDC members who had been arrested and mistreated by another Chilean security service offered small hope that he would use his influence to end abuses. In retrospect, however, Contreras' role in this effort probably reflected interservice rivalry and Contreras' personal efforts to control the entire Chilean intelligence apparatus.

By April 1975, intelligence reporting showed that Contreras was the principal obstacle to a reasonable human rights policy within the Junta, but an interagency committee directed the CIA to continue its relationship with Contreras. The US Ambassador to Chile urged Deputy Director of Central Intelligence Walters to receive Contreras in Washington in the interest of maintaining good relations with Pinochet. In August 1975, with interagency approval, this meeting took place.

In May and June 1975, elements within the CIA recommended establishing a paid relationship with Contreras to obtain intelligence based on his unique position and access to Pinochet. This proposal was overruled, citing the US Government policy on clandestine relations with the head of an intelligence service notorious for human rights abuses. However, given miscommunications in the timing of this exchange, a one-time payment was given to Contreras.

In addition to information concerning external threats, CIA sought from Contreras information regarding evidence that emerged in 1975 of a formal Southern Cone cooperative intelligence effort—"Operation Condor"—building on informal cooperation in tracking and, in at least a few cases, killing political opponents. By October 1976 there was sufficient information that the CIA decided to approach Contreras on the matter. Contreras confirmed Condor's existence as an intelligence-sharing network but denied that it had a role in extra-judicial killings.

Former Allende cabinet member and Ambassador to Washington Orlando Letelier and his American assistant, Ronni Moffit, were killed in a carbombing in Washington on 21 September, 1976. Almost immediately after the assassination, rumors began circulating that the Chilean government was responsible. CIA's first intelligence report containing this allegation was dated 6 October 1976. During October 1976, the Department of Justice and the CIA worked out how the CIA would support the foreign intelligence (FI) aspects of the legal investigation. At that time, Contreras' possible role in the Letelier assassination became an issue.

By the end of 1976, contacts with Contreras were very infrequent. During 1977, CIA met with Contreras about half a dozen times; three of those contacts were to request information on the Letelier assassination. On 3 November 1977, Contreras was transferred to a function unrelated to intelligence so CIA severed all contact with him.

Nonetheless, CIA intelligence reporting continued to follow Contreras' activities closely. After a short struggle to retain power, Contreras resigned from the Army in 1978. In the interim, CIA gathered specific, detailed intelligence reporting concerning Contreras' involvement in ordering the Letelier assassination. While some of this material has been released, some remains classified and another portion has been withheld at the request of the Department of Justice, which continues to pursue the investigation.

The CIA Reported on Abuses but Took No Action

Throughout the post-coup period, the CIA collected and disseminated to the intelligence and policy communities extensive reporting concerning human rights issues in Chile. Some of this information came from contacts with mixed reputations. The intelligence included a wide variety of information, including:

- Debates in 1973–88 within the Chilean military and security services about the appropriate level of force to be used in confronting what they viewed as the subversive threat posed by leftist political groups and splinter terrorist organizations;
- The identities and activities of sub-units within the Chilean security forces charged with conducting special political activities or activities against the left, and whose association with extremist groups with violent tendencies made them most prone to systemic abuses;
- Debates within leftist political groups and splinter terrorist organizations concerning the use of violence in confronting the government; and
- Training, capabilities, readiness and deployment of the various "self-defense" groups within the Socialist and Communist Parties of Chile and splinter terrorist organizations of the Movement of the Revolutionary Left, the Manuel Rodriguez Patriotic Front and the Lautaro Youth and Worker/Peasant factions of the United Popular Action Movement.

In the days and months immediately following the 1973 coup, the CIA provided extensive reporting on what the government characterized as activities necessary to restore order. There were widely varying reports on the numbers of persons killed and arrested. CIA reporting confirmed that the military was deliberately not disclosing accurate figures and detailed the differing opinions within the military Junta regarding whether to summarily execute extremists and subversives or allow them trials and sentencing. There was also extensive reporting on:

- Application of "military justice" to civilian detainees and the types of punishment they were likely to face;
- Prison camp locations and the names of specific persons being held in them, including the fact that some of these locations were secret;
- Efforts of leftists to flee the country or gain asylum in foreign embassies; and
- Assessments of the effect government repression was having on the left's capabilities and efforts to regroup.

CIA also received information on "Plan Z"—purportedly drawn up by Allende's Popular Unity coalition in the late period of the Allende Government to assassinate important political and military persons opposed to its leftist agenda. When allegations of the existence of "Plan Z" first surfaced, the CIA noted that it probably was disinformation manipulated by the Junta to improve its image and to provide justification for its activities. Allegations that reports about "Plan Z" were part of a joint CIA-Chilean operation are inaccurate, although military officers with whom the CIA had contact prior to the 1973 coup were involved in the drafting the "White Book," in which allegations of "Plan Z" were a main feature.

The CIA first reported human rights abuses by the Junta on 15 September 1973, just days after the coup. CIA reported that the Chilean security interrogation units were dealing with suspected opponents in an extremely rigorous manner. A 22 September report noted that prisoners at the National Stadium were harshly treated in the first days after the coup. On 28 September, CIA reported that 27 cadavers, some showing signs of torture and mutilation, had been recovered from the Mapocho River. On 9 October, the CIA reported that Soviet non-diplomatic technicians in Chile had been repeatedly threatened and verbally abused; some of those later tried were beaten or injured. On 25 October, CIA reported that General Sergio Arellano Stark had given instructions resulting in the summary execution of 21 political prisoners. On 3 November, the CIA reported that, despite a government decree to end summary executions, 20 bodies were found shot in the San Carlos Canal. On 12 November, the CIA reported concerns within the PDC about human rights abuses. On 18 January 1974, CIA reported that Chilean politicians across the political spectrum were weighing the possibility of bringing the issue of government human rights abuses to the attention of the United Nations Commission on Human Rights.

It was apparent that the 17 January 1974 Chilean government circular prohibiting torture and providing instructions for the handling of prisoners was a public relations ruse. CIA reporting indicated that the Chilean security forces did not, and probably would not, observe the stated policy. Although the State Department and Embassy had the primary role in human rights reporting, the clandestine nature of Chilean security services' human rights practices required CIA collection efforts. In late January 1974, the CIA directed that all appropriate CIA officers task their clandestine assets to report on torture in Chile.

Over the next 17 years, the CIA reported information available from its contacts concerning human rights abuses in Chile. As the left later regained strength, intelligence reporting included the plans, intentions, capabilities and terrorist acts of the left. During the transition from military to civilian rule, intelligence reporting followed the political issue of how human rights investigations and prosecutions would be handled.

A review of CIA's files has uncovered no evidence that CIA officers and employees were engaged in human rights abuses or in covering up any human rights abuses in Chile.

CIA Involvement in the Death/Disappearance of US Citizens

Allegations of CIA complicity in the death of American citizen Charles Horman, Jr—an expatriate who supported Allende and was murdered in the aftermath of the coup in 1973—are unfounded. Similarly, CIA had no prior knowledge of the circumstances leading to the death in Chile of US citizen Frank Teruggi in 1973 or the disappearance of US citizen Boris Weisfeiler in 1985.

Nevertheless, some clandestine contacts of the CIA were involved in human rights abuses. The CIA, at the direction of and with the full concurrence of senior US policymakers, maintained official contacts with various security services. At the same time, the CIA maintained clandestine contacts with selected members of the Chilean military, intelligence and security forces, both to collect intelligence and carry out the covert actions described above. There is no doubt that some CIA contacts were actively engaged in committing and covering up serious human rights abuses.

As a result of lessons learned in Chile, Central America and elsewhere, the CIA now carefully reviews all contacts for potential involvement in human rights abuses and makes a deliberate decision balancing the nature and severity of the human rights abuse against the potential intelligence value of continuing the relationship. These standards, established in the mid-1990s, would likely have altered the amount of contact we had with perpetrators of human rights violators in Chile had they been in effect at that time.

Viewpoint 6

On His Ninety-First Birthday Pinochet Takes "Political Responsibility"

Augusto Pinochet

On the occasion of his ninety-first birthday in 1996, Augusto Pinochet wrote the following viewpoint—a letter that the general instructed his wife to read aloud publicly for the media. In it Pinochet makes skirting reference to the 1973 coup when he led the Chilean army to overthrow President Salvador Allende's democratically elected Marxist government. Similarly he vaguely notes the violence and alleged crimes against humanity that followed. Twice in the course of the letter Pinochet takes "political responsibility" for everything that happened under his government. Pinochet's supporters as well as victims of his regime, the international press, and legal scholars continue to debate what, precisely, this admission meant. Pinochet died less than a month after releasing the letter, however, without ever standing trial for humanitarian crimes. Chilean army general and dictator Augusto Pinochet was president of Chile from 1973 to 1990.

Dear Friends,

I thank all of you, through my dear wife, for the affection that you have shown me on my birthday.

Augusto Pinochet, "Carta de Augusto Pinochet con Motivo de Su Cumpleaños Número 91," *El Mercurio*, accessed December 20, 2012. Translation by David Erik Nelson. From es.wikisource.org.

Ninety-one years ago I was born in this marvelous land. Life imposed upon me hard duties that I had to meet thinking only of the well-being of Chile and its children. Civil strife, unprovoked by the military, obligated us to act in defense of liberty, law, and democracy, in a tumultuous world in which the fate of all mankind was debated.

I should thank God for giving me a wife that has accompanied me and given me the necessary strength to confront the rigors of my destiny; for having been able to see my children, grandchildren, and great-grandchildren grow up in a free, powerful, modern, and admired nation; and for having avoided a fratricidal confrontation, guiding Chile back to the path of liberty and law.

The Chile we built after 1973, with everyone's sacrifice, has left behind the totalitarian threat. It has projected us toward a higher destiny, giving us a better tomorrow and a higher, more just, standard of living. The sacrifices made have been worthwhile.

Lucia Hiriart de Pinochet, Augusto Pinochet's wife, reads the letter sent to his supporters on his ninety-first birthday in 2006. © David Lillo/AFP/Getty Images.

Today, near the end of my days, I want to state that I do not hold a grudge against anyone, that I love my fatherland above all, and that I take political responsibility for everything that's been done, with the conviction that no other path could have so exalted Chile and prevented its disintegration.

I especially want to give a message of support to my comrades-in-arms, many of them prisoners, who suffer the persecution and revenge of those who unleashed the civic unrest and violence that obliged the armed forces and police to intervene and triumph in a fight that seemed insurmountable. Thanks to their courage and determination, Chile was able to transition from a totalitarian menace to the full democracy that we restored, and which all of our compatriots now enjoy. If after thirty years those who provoked chaos and the confrontation have been restored and reintroduced to the rule of law, then it is not fitting to demand punishment for those that prevented the spreading and deepening of the worst political, moral, economic, and national identity crisis within memory. I reiterate what I have always said: I assume the full political responsibility for what happened.

All of the taunting, persecution, and injustice that has affected me and my family, I offer myself to these gladly for the sake of the harmony and peace that ought to rein among the people of Chile.

I have absolute certainty that tomorrow, when these passions and resentments are at an end, history will judge our work objectively and recognize that the work done here placed Chile at the head of the nations of this continent.

I pray to Divine Providence that we are able to overcome the injuries that are inevitably left behind by political and social upheavals like that which we confronted in 1973, and which reestablished in Chile unity, harmony, and peace. Only then will we return to being great and bury our hatred and *revanchismo* [desire to return to a previous political status quo].

Much thanks to all of you for the loyalty and gratitude that has sustained this old soldier, upon whose watch the Nation was placed in a historic dilemma that we managed to resolve with the support and backing of your comrades-in-arms and the heroic people of Chile.

LONG LIVE CHILE.

Chapter 2

Controversies Surrounding Chile Under Augusto Pinochet

Chapter Exercises

Bye Bye Pinochet. © Patrick Chappatte, Le Temps, Switzerland.

1. Analyze the Cartoon

Question 1: Who is in the casket? What clues to the person's identity did the artist include in the drawing itself?

Question 2: Who or what do the people shown behind the pallbearers represent? What are they doing and what might they want to achieve with their actions?

Question 3: Is the depiction of the dead person and the funeral positive, negative, or neutral? What feelings or opinions do you think the artist wanted to convey?

2. Writing Prompt

Assume the role of an American newspaper editor in the 1980s and write an editorial bringing attention to the plight of women and girls arrested during Pinochet's regime. What actions should you urge US readers to take?

3. Group Activity

Break into groups and debate the involvement of the United States regarding Augusto Pinochet's regime. Was the CIA's covert support of Pinochet justified? Was it wise? What responsibility do US citizens have for actions taken in their name and with their financial support? Does it matter if these actions are taken without their explicit knowledge or permission?

Viewpoint 1

Pinochet's Actions in Chile Constitute "Political Genocide"

Maureen S. Hiebert and Pablo Policzer

The following viewpoint examines an ongoing debate surrounding the legal definition of genocide (as worded by the UN Convention on the Punishment and Prevention of the Crime of Genocide) when applied to the killing of individuals targeted for their political affiliations. Determining whether these cases of "politicide" are lesser atrocities than genocide is especially important in the case of Chile under Augusto Pinoche's regime. The authors address this dispute and argue that politicide should be considered a form of genocide. Maureen S. Hiebert is assistant professor of political science and law and society at the University of Calgary, Alberta. Pablo Policzer is professor of Latin American politics at the University of Calgary and the author of The Rise and Fall of Repression in Chile.

Did the Chilean military dictatorship commit genocide? The dictatorship, which overthrew the left-wing government of Salvador Allende in 1973 and ruled for the next 17 years, killed members of political opposition groups, as well as those

From: "Genocide in Chile? An Assessment," *State Violence and Genocide in Latin America: The Cold War Years,* Maureen Hiebert and Pablo Policzer, eds. Marcia Esparza, Henry R. Huttenbach, and Daniel Feierstein. Copyright © 2011 Taylor & Francis Books UK. Reproduced by permission of Taylor & Francis Books UK.

it suspected of sympathizing with such groups. Chile's Truth and Reconciliation Commission Report (known as the *Informe Rettig* and published in 1991), documented some 3,200 victims killed by the dictatorship; yet it avoided using the term genocide. In Argentina, the Report of the National Commission on the Disappearance of Persons (CONADEP), which documented some 9,000 victims, also avoided it; yet in that country the accusation of genocide is gaining increasingly wide acceptance in official documents and sources. Should the same happen in Chile?

Understanding "Political" Genocide

Chile is an ambiguous case because state directed killing in and of itself does not necessarily constitute genocide. Further, the victims in Chile were primarily political actors and groups rather than ethnic, "racial," national, or religious groups as has been the case in most genocides. To evaluate whether the political killings in Chile may be considered genocidal we must review the debates in the literature on genocide studies over how to define genocide and how these debates can help illuminate the status of the Chilean case.

Like others in the social sciences, genocide is a highly contested concept about which scholars in the field continue to strongly disagree. Unlike most social science concepts (with the exception of those in law and criminology), genocide is also a legally codified crime in international and domestic law. It has also become a normative label that victims of human rights abuses wield to draw attention to their suffering, and that perpetrators deny in their own efforts to neutralize accusations that they have committed the most heinous of crimes. It is for these reasons that there is no one widely accepted definition of genocide against which we can measure the Chilean experience. Rather, we must evaluate the Chilean case in the context of three key debates in the literature over how to define genocide. These debates revolve around: the identity of the victim group (who are the victims of genocide?), the intention of the perpetrators (does genocide require a specific "intent to destroy"?), and the extent and methods of destruction (is there a numerical or proportional threshold of destruction and/or manner of destruction that is unique to genocide?). Our review of these debates suggests that the violence directed by the Chilean regime against its opponents was closer to genocide than commonly assumed.

Violence Targeting a Political Ideology

The most obvious grounds upon which we might disqualify Chile as a case of genocide is the identity of the victim group, insofar as the targets of the regime were political groups (members of left-wing parties and movements), and not ethnic, national, or religious groups. The 1948 United Nations Convention on the Punishment and Prevention of the Crime of Genocide (UNGC) and some noted genocide scholars exclude political groups from their definitions because these groups are considered to be too amorphous and transitory. The UNGC stipulates that genocide is the "attempt to destroy" four specific kinds of groups: "national, ethnical, racial, and religious groups as such." Political groups are obviously absent from this list. When it was being negotiated, the Soviet and Iranian delegations argued for leaving political groups out of the final draft of the UNGC. It was this position, adopted largely to prevent the Convention from being scuttled, which ruled the day. For the Soviets, genocide was not applicable to political groups because they understood genocide as a crime inherent to Nazism, a fundamentally race-based ideology and political system. The Soviet delegation further argued that from a "'socialist scientific' perspective political groups do not have identifiable 'objective characteristics' as do racial or ethnic groups."...

Scholars who reject the idea that the victimization of political groups can be genocidal argue that not only are political groups mutable, but also that they are targeted for political or ideological reasons. Therefore, the use of violence against them, while obviously wrong, constitutes human rights violations such as the safety and security of the person, freedom of expression, assembly and the like, but not genocide. Manus Midlarsky, for example, argues that genocide involves the "systematic mass murder of people based on ethnoreligious identity" only, because this kind of killing "tap[s] into much deeper historical roots of the human condition" than does the targeting of "designated enemies of the state based on socioeconomic or political criteria." Political or socioeconomic victims of state-sponsored mass murder, he argues, are "attributable to more detailed ideological considerations."

Distinguishing "Politicide" from Genocide

Analysts like Midlarsky follow Barbara Harff's contention that the victimization of political and socioeconomic groups constitutes a separate but related phenomenon to genocide called "politicide." For Harff, both genocides and politicides are characterized by the intent to destroy "a communal, political, or politicized ethnic group." The difference between genocide and politicide rests on how the perpetrators define the identity of the victim group. In genocide the victim groups are identified by the perpetrator along "communal characteristics," while in politicides "groups are defined primarily in terms of their political opposition to the regime and dominant group."

Although the preceding understanding of genocide would seem to preclude the Chilean case, it is important to remember that the original formulation of the crime of genocide by the Polish-American jurist Raphael Lemkin, along with the work of many contemporary genocidal scholars, suggests that political groups are essentially no different than the more "primordial" victim groups commonly associated with genocide. Moreover, the historical record shows that radical regimes have not been shy about targeting their political opponents, real and imagined, for genocidal destruction. For Lemkin, genocide included the extermination of groups "because of their political beliefs and/or practices." The 1946 United National General Assembly

Leftist Political Groups in Chile

Before the coup of 1973, Salvador Allende was the democratically elected, Marxist president of Chile. Allende's political party—the "Popular Unity" party, or *Unidad Popular* (UP)—was actually a coalition of several left-leaning political groups in Chile. These groups included:

- The Socialist Party (which was cofounded by Allende)
- The Communist Party
- The Radical Party (a moderate center-left party founded in 1863)
- The Popular Unitary Action Movement (a youth-oriented group that splintered from the Christian Democrats)
- The Christian Left (a leftist splinter from the Christian Democrats)
- The Party of the Radical Left (now called the Party of Social Democracy, a more leftist offshoot of the Radical Party)
- The Christian Democrats (a centrist party that frequently bridged capitalist and communist ideologies)

In 1973 the coalition's support from the Christian Democrats made it possible for the narrowly elected Allende to take power. During a congressional protest in August of 1973, however, the Christian Democrats shifted their support to the right-wing National Party, setting the stage for Augusto Pinochet's rise to power.

Another group supporting the Popular Unity coalition was the far-left paramilitary organization called the Revolutionary Left Movement, or *Movimiento de Izquierda Revolucionaria* (MIR). The MIR clashed with right-wing paramilitary groups prior to the coup and fought against the Chilean military both during the coup and in its aftermath. Pinochet's new government, however, outlawed all of the parties associated with the Popular Unity coalition (apart from the Christian Democrats), often reserving the most violent reprisals for members of the MIR.

Resolution 96 (I) calling on member states to draw up a convention to prevent and punish genocide included the assertion that "[m]any instances of such crimes of genocide have occurred when racial, religious, political, and other groups have been destroyed, entirely or in part."

"Politicide" Is a Form of Genocide

The ultimate exclusion of political and socioeconomic groups from the final version of the 1948 UNGC was not because genocide by its nature only involves communal groups into which individuals are born. While the Soviet, Iranian and other delegations argued otherwise, most Western states, including the United States, supported the inclusion of political groups, noting that membership in such groups was no more mutable than in religious groups, and that history has shown that states have been "easily able to identify political groups they wished to destroy." Before being voted off the Convention at Soviet insistence, political groups remained in successive drafts of the Convention until 29 November 1948. Political groups were recognized in these drafts as victims of genocide with the caveat that the Convention was only applicable "to the most horrible form of crime against a group, that of physical destruction." Western and other delegations that supported the inclusion of political groups relented to the Soviet position not because of the latter's superior logic, but as a matter of political expediency to save the Convention, imperfect though it was.

Following on some of the debates presented at the UN when the UNGC was being negotiated, scholars who support the recognition of political groups have not only reiterated the idea that there is no objective difference between political and communal groups—since both the latter and the former categories can be constructed by the members themselves and the perpetrators of genocidal killing—but they also argue that ideological motivation is not a credible basis upon which to exclude political groups. [F.R.] Chalk and [K.] Jonassohn, for example, note that although political and socioeconomic groups have been targeted for destruction based on ideologically derived conceptions of the victims as "enemies of the people," these alleged enemies "are mythical to begin with" and, therefore, "it is futile to search for rational and objective boundaries to define them. . . . Millions of human beings have died because of their alleged membership in these 'mutable' groups.". . .

Political Genocide in Chile

Our aim in this brief essay has not been to document the extent to which genocide occurred in Chile, but to suggest how it may be possible to begin to think about whether it did or not. By contrast to Argentina, where the claim of genocide has been increasingly accepted in official circles, the Chilean case continues to be understood as one of massive human rights violations and political violence (including detentions, torture, killings, and disappearances), but not genocide. Our assessment of how scholars understand the phenomenon of genocide suggests that the Chilean regime's crimes should be reconsidered. While it is a less obvious case of genocide than others in Latin America (such as Guatemala, where large numbers of victims were targeted because of their identity as members of indigenous communities, or Argentina, where a larger number of political opponents were killed than in Chile, often using "root and branch" methods), it demonstrates both the clear intention to eliminate a specific group of political opponents deemed to be a threat to national security, and their deliberate and purposeful targeting in order to achieve this outcome.

Viewpoint 2

Doctors Voluntarily Participated in Torture Under the Pinochet Regime

British Medical Association

The following viewpoint is an excerpt of Medicine Betrayed: The Participation of Doctors in Human Rights Abuses, *a book-length 1992 report produced by the British Medical Association (BMA) in 1992. The sections on Augusto Pinochet's regime demonstrate the high degree to which doctors were integrated into its torture practice. The association reports that these practices included medical screening of prisoners prior to torture, the presence of doctors during torture and interrogation sessions, medical examinations and treatment following torture, and at times false certification of injuries or causes of death. The authors argue that the significance of these actions spread beyond medical involvement in torture, indicating a larger culture of acquiescence despite such brutality. The BMA is a professional group representing doctors in the United Kingdom. Its medical ethics committee is widely recognized as one of the foremost authorities on ethical medical practices.*

Doctors and other medical personnel can get involved in serious violations of human rights at any point in the process. While doctors are not trained in a culture of strict obedience as are

British Medical Association, *Medicine Betrayed: The Participation of Doctors in Human Rights Abuses*. London: Zed Books, 1992, pp. 43–63.

military personnel, some doctors work within a milieu where security considerations take high priority. Those who are most likely to assist in human rights abuses are the medical personnel who are directly responsible for examining and providing health care for prisoners. Some are dragged into this role by enforced conscription into military service where they can find themselves called upon to treat tortured "enemy" prisoners (whether internal opposition or external army). Even doctors who normally have no contact with detained individuals can find themselves involved with those who have been tortured or who are at risk of torture by, for example, the admission of an ill-treated detainee to a general hospital. Some doctors, who initially join the army freely, become entangled in activities which breach internationally accepted medical standards. This was graphically described by the Chilean witness . . . who had joined the army as a young doctor just prior to the September 1973 military coup, and subsequently found himself a horrified witness to a multiple extrajudicial execution:

> I was called on one occasion to go to a seaside resort to examine some prisoners who were to be transferred to Concepción. I examined the prisoners and I felt that they were fit to travel. On the way back [to Concepción] the convoy stopped and I was told to remain in the jeep. Shortly afterwards I heard some shots, I tried to get out but they forced me back in. I then literally forced my way out. I remember this more as a nightmare. I believe that some of the people or all of the people were shot there.

Although this doctor had felt shocked and believed that these executions were an outrage into which he had been drawn against his will, he knew that there was no one in authority to whom he could turn, and that he was powerless to stop similar incidents happening in the future. He attempted to discuss the subject with other young doctors in the same position but found them intimidated and unwilling to discuss it or take any action. In explaining to the [British Medical Association] Working Party what ultimately prevented him from conforming to the reluctant practice of his peers, he indicated that much had hinged on having some external advice and support. Without this, he felt he might well have lost his moral perspective and obeyed his officers. After placing himself at some risk on several occasions, his "obstinacy" led to his being dismissed from the army and subsequently he went into exile. The problem of isolation is a considerable one, since no professional machinery currently exists to provide support to doctors attempting to combat abuses of human rights in situations of serious personal risk. . . .

Our consideration of the evidence for medical involvement in torture is broken down into the following: examinations prior to torture; presence, examination or treatment during torture; medical examination or treatment after torture; false certification after torture. Some prisoners, of course, have the misfortune to meet hostile or unhelpful medical personnel at several points throughout their stay in detention.

Examination Prior to Torture

The role of the doctor in examining prisoners entering a place of detention is potentially a protective factor in the prisoner's interests. Indeed, Amnesty International called for such examinations as one of its "12 Point Program for the Prevention of Torture" which was published in 1984 and incorporated in the BMA [British Medical Association] *Torture Report* of 1986. The same provision has been adopted in international human rights instruments. For example, the Body of Principles for the Protection of All Persons under Any Form of Detention or Imprisonment (1988) specifies at principle 24 that:

> A proper medical examination shall be offered to a detained or imprisoned person as promptly as possible after his admission to the place of detention or imprisonment, and thereafter medical care and treatment shall be provided whenever necessary . . . .

However, as [M] Phillips and [J] Dawson have noted:

> [There appears to be] a clear distinction to be drawn between the doctor acting on behalf of the prisoner and at his request, and acting on behalf of the administration. In the former role, a doctor is acting entirely properly in attending to need and alleviating distress; in the latter, however, he is not only part of the process that is causing the distress but by virtue of his professional standing he is lending that process some spurious respectability since he appears to condone it. . . . The problem is that in practice it is extremely difficult to separate the two. Examining a prisoner before he is tortured is more straight forward, since the only reason for such an examination is to pronounce the prisoner fit to undergo duress and therefore must be wrong. But examining the prisoner afterwards provokes the dilemma, since it could be in the prisoner's interest or in the interest of the torturers. . . . In practice, however, it is extremely unlikely that any doctor allowed to examine a prisoner in such circumstances would be a free agent, and that his treatment and opinion would not be used by the torturers.

Indeed, there is much evidence to suggest that doctors or other medical staff who examine prisoners do not always act with the necessary clinical independence and in fact sometimes actively collaborate with security or police in the torture of prisoners.

Chilean Doctors "Approved" Prisoners for Torture

In Chile, during the government of Augusto Pinochet, there was abundant evidence that doctors examined prisoners on entry into the secret detention centres of the *Central National de Informaciones* (CNI, the Chilean security police). The nature of the examination, which appeared to note conditions which could be seriously aggravated by torture, suggested (and subsequent events confirmed) that the main function of the medical examination was to allow for "effective" torture. For example, a man arrested in Arica in the north of Chile in 1983 alleged:

> I was again taken to the first room, undressed and examined by the doctor, who even measured my blood pressure. . . . Then another interrogation expert, I think, came in and asked, "Have you examined this one yet? Is he good for a going over?" The answer was affirmative.

The same pattern occurred in other Chilean cities:

> A male detainee arrested [in Valparaiso in October 1983] alleged that he had been asked by "someone who appeared to be a doctor" about previous illnesses, about the symptoms and about the medication he was taking. After examining him with a stethoscope and asking him if he suffered from asthma, he called out that [the detainee] could take it.

An investigation into medical involvement in torture in Chile carried out by the Colegio Médico de Chile found that the role of the doctor in the work of the security police was highly developed. According to a report published by the Colegio Médico in 1986:

> One physician who had worked for the security forces told us that there was an entire clinical structure in place with specialists, resources, shifts, joint consulting, and even 'emergency calls' to respond to any imprudence or over-zealous action by other officials that put the life of a detainee in danger. It should be understood that these 'emergency services' are provided to those patients who, because of their deteriorated physical or mental state, are often unable to request their own medical attention.
>
> As our investigations continued, we discovered that physicians working within this system had medically examined detainees before torture and then issued certificates of good health after torture.

Unfortunately, the return to democracy in Chile has not put an end to allegations of torture and of medical involvement. In September 1991, Amnesty International reported that more than

The Hidden Side of the Dictatorship. © Osmani Simanca, Brazil, www.caglecartoons.com.

30 complaints of torture had been submitted to Chilean courts since the coming to power of the Aylwin government in March 1990. . . .

Presence, Examination, or Treatment During Torture

The most charitable interpretation one can put on the presence of medical personnel during the interrogation of a prisoner is that they are there to ensure the interrogation doesn't go "too far". . . .

The overwhelming body of evidence of medical participation in torture indicates that the role of the doctor is not to guarantee a humanitarian presence to help save the prisoner from the excessive enthusiasm of dedicated interrogators; rather the doctor is there to support the torturers. In some cases the testimony given by prisoners suggests a reluctance on the part of the doctor to play the role assigned to him or perhaps an attempt to offer some small assistance to the prisoner. In other cases, the doctor is reported to play a consistent and malevolent role.

Continuing allegations of torture in Chile include isolated reports of apparent medical involvement. A man arrested by the *Carabineros* [police] in Santiago on 9 August 1990 alleged that he was given electric shocks to the genitals, chest and feet, and subjected to *submarino* [prolonged drinking], as well as other forms of torture. He alleged that, while under torture, he was examined by a woman performing medical duties, following which torture continued. . . .

Medical Examination or Treatment of Prisoners After Torture

After a session of severe torture, the prisoner may require immediate medical attention to save his or her life. Evidence made available to the Working Party made clear that doctors assisting victims of torture after they have been removed from the torture chamber acted with a variety of motives. The obligation to provide treatment when requested or in case of emergency applies equally in the case of the torture victim. However, three ethical factors come into play in such a situation—at least in principle. The first is that the doctor is enjoined by the Declaration of Tokyo not to condone or tolerate the torture and is thus obliged to note the torture and report it. Secondly, the doctor must pay due attention to the consent of the prisoner to any treatment the doctor proposes. This may require the doctor to be sensitive to a desire by the prisoner to refuse treatment because of the unbearable suffering he or she is being subjected to (though of course it may be impossible for the prisoner to express any coherent view in the circumstances). Thirdly, the doctor must assess the best interests of the prisoner and recommend measures which coincide with those best interests. The return of the prisoner to a prison cell and to the control of military personnel clearly is not in the prisoner's best interests though the doctor may be in a very weak position to influence the decision concerning the prisoner's fate. . . .

Civilian Doctors Supporting Government Torture Programs

In most countries, it is those doctors working in prisons and other places of detention, police surgeons, who assist in forensic aspects of police work and military doctors, who may be required to work with detained soldiers and prisoners of war, who are most likely to confront the issue of ill-treatment and torture. Where doctors in such institutions are isolated, or have worked for many years in the same institution, or work under the overriding responsibility of the prison authorities, there is a risk of their independence, and capacity to assert their ethical principles, being diminished. If the doctor is "one of the boys"—a functionary dependent on officer colleagues for friendship or good will, or to civil superiors for professional advancement—then there is a basis for exerting considerable pressure on them not to be obstructive, or possibly to actively assist the torture to go "smoothly".

In addition, these are precisely the doctors who are most likely to be required to observe some form of "contract of obedience". A doctor faced with a choice between a moral oath and a military oath may find the conflict extremely difficult to resolve. . . .

If police, prison and military doctors are most likely to be the personnel seeing tortured prisoners, they are not the only ones. During widespread military operations, it is possible for local doctors to be asked to provide medical services, including to prisoners. Equally, doctors working in hospital casualty departments or intensive care units may also find themselves dealing with serious trauma inflicted on a prisoner. In a notorious Chilean case, a seriously ill prisoner, Federico Alvarez Santibañez, was transferred from the custody of the security police to the Penitentiary Hospital where a medical student recorded:

> Multiple contusions on the cranium, thorax and extremities. Pallid, rapid and shallow breathing, pain in sternum, multiple thoracic pains, nausea, heavy perspiration, labored breathing. Lucid and oriented. Extensive bruising around the eye sockets.

His condition worsened and he was transferred to another specialist hospital where he died. The day of his transfer from security police custody:

> He was "examined" by Dr Luis Losada Fuenzalida in his capacity as a CNI [security police] physician. It is obvious that Dr Losada placed the interest of the CNI before . . . his patient's because the health certificate he signed reads as follows: "The undersigned physician has professionally examined Federico Renato Alvarez Santibañez, C.I. 646.500-8 of Santiago, and found him in good health and showing no wounds of any kind. Santiago, 20 May 1979." In May 1986, the Chilean Medical Association expelled Dr Losada. . . .

Investigating and Punishing Medical Involvement in Torture

Torture is illegal under international law and frequently prohibited by the laws applying in countries where it is practised. It is not surprising therefore that attempts are made to hide it. In addition, those who have been tortured may not want to report their experiences, either because of the suffering this may cause or because they feel that publicising their story may put others at risk. . . .

In Chile, the *Colegio Médico* (Medical Association) has pursued a cautious and confidential path towards the investigation and disciplining of doctors found to be involved in torture. Since 1983, the association has undertaken enquiries regarding the alleged participation of 12 doctors. Investigations regarding a 13th doctor opened in March 1991 though, according to Dr Gunter Seelman of the medical association, this last doctor has left Chile apparently to avoid further investigations. To date, six doctors have been penalised, three of whom have been expelled from the

College and three temporarily suspended. Again this is a small number considering the long period in which torture was practised with extreme brutality and lack of restraint, and in which doctors appear to have been heavily involved. . . .

The weight of evidence available to the Working Party was such as to allow no other conclusion than that the problem of medical participation, tolerance or cover-up of torture is persistent in some countries and an occasional problem in others. The numbers of doctors involved is impossible to estimate due to the secret and illegal nature of the abuse. In very many cases, there is little evidence that the doctors took any feasible measure to avoid involvement or protect the victim. For such cases, the Working Party has no hesitation in expressing its extreme repugnance of the doctor's behaviour and supporting calls for disciplinary hearings. We believe that the medical profession, and particularly medical associations, must take a more active stand against such unethical and unacceptable behaviour. In doing so, it will need to take into account the need to balance the obligation to report the torture with the need to protect the patient. Clearly, this is an area where medical confidentiality is of the utmost importance.

Tolerating Torture Within the Wider Medical Community

Nevertheless, the Working Party felt that focusing *only* on the doctors directly involved in gross abuses risks missing the wider perspective both of medical a*cquiescence in,* or *tolerance of,* torture (by, for example, professional indifference, fear or lack of knowledge of possible measures).

The Working Party also felt it important to draw attention to medical acceptance or involvement in practices which may fall short of torture in the strict sense of the word but which are nevertheless unethical and may be cruel, inhuman or degrading.

While torture and medical involvement in torture will most frequently occur within places of detention or interrogation, knowledge of torture spreads much further. Of equal or greater importance, there is inevitably a wider pattern of abuses than outright torture, particularly in democratic states where checks operate against the worse excesses, and it is important that this phenomenon also be addressed. In some ways medical acquiescence in these types of abuse risks being insidious as it does not provoke the widespread and focused response that reports of medical involvement in torture do.

Although there is currently an abundance of ethical statements and principles available to the profession to address the subject of torture, there is a relative lack of concrete actions which can be brought into play to assist the doctor faced with having to resist pressure to assist in torture. More importantly, there remains the need to develop concrete and feasible measures which states and medical bodies can implement to *prevent* doctors being placed in situations where such choices have to be contemplated.

Viewpoint 3

Pinochet's Tactics Were Justified by the Threat of Totalitarianism in Latin America

George Reisman

The following viewpoint was originally part of a set of essays published by the Ludwig von Mises Institute soon after Augusto Pinochet's death in December 2006. The institute is a think tank whose mission is "to place human choice at the center of economic theory . . . through the defense of the market economy, private property, sound money, and peaceful international relations, while opposing government intervention as economically and socially destructive." In the following viewpoint, the author defends Pinochet's legacy and actions—even at their most extreme. Primarily he applauds Pinochet's success in preventing the spread of communism into the western hemisphere. He then lauds Pinochet for greatly expanding economic freedom in Chile and paving the way for an orderly transition back to functional democracy. The author goes on to explain why Pinochet's seemingly harsh treatment of Salvador Allende, his supporters, and left-leaning citizens was a reasonable and proportionate response to the threat of a socialist regime. George Reisman, Ph.D., is the author of Capitalism: A Treatise

George Reisman, "General Augusto Pinochet Is Dead" and "More on Pinochet and Marxism: The Necessity of Evil Means to Achieve Socialism," Ludwig von Mises Institute website, December 16 and 21, 2006. www.mises.org.

on Economics *and Pepperdine University Emeritus Professor of Economics.*

On Sunday, December 10 [2006], General Augusto Pinochet of Chile died, at the age of 91. General Pinochet deserves to be remembered for having rescued his country from becoming the second Soviet satellite in the Western hemisphere, after Castro's Cuba, and, like the Soviet Union, and Cuba under Castro, a totalitarian dictatorship.

Pinochet's Actions Were Justified by the Political Realities of the Period

The General is denounced again and again for the death or disappearance of over 3,000 Chilean citizens and the alleged torture of thousands more. It may well be that some substantial number of innocent Chilean citizens did die or disappear or otherwise suffered brutal treatment as the result of his actions. But in a struggle to avoid the establishment of a Communist dictatorship, it is undoubtedly true that many or most of those who died or suffered were preparing to inflict a far greater number of deaths and a vastly larger scale of suffering on their fellow citizens.

Their deaths and suffering should certainly not be mourned, any more than the deaths of Lenin, Stalin, and Hitler, and their helpers should be mourned. Had there been a General Pinochet in Russia in 1918 or Germany in 1933, the people of those countries and of the rest of the world would have been incomparably better off, precisely by virtue of the death, disappearance, and attendant suffering of vast numbers of Communists and Nazis. Life and liberty are positively helped by the death and disappearance of such mortal enemies. Their absence from the scene means the absence of such things as concentration camps, and is thus ardently to be desired.

As for the innocent victims in Chile, their fate should overwhelmingly be laid at the door of the Communist plotters of totalitarian dictatorship. People have an absolute right to rise up and defend their lives, liberty, and property against a Communist takeover. In the process, they cannot be expected to make the distinctions present in a judicial process. They must act quickly and decisively to remove what threatens them. That is the nature of war. The fate of innocent bystanders, largely those who cannot be readily distinguished from the enemy, is the responsibility of the Communists. Had they not attempted to impose their totalitarian dictatorship, there would not have been any need to use force and violence to prevent them, and thus the innocent would not have suffered.

Contrary to the attitude of so many of today's intellectuals, Communists do not have a right to murder tens of millions of innocent people and then to complain when their intended victims prevent their takeover and in the process kill some of them.

Pinochet Was a Uniquely Virtuous Dictator

General Pinochet was undoubtedly no angel. No soldier can be. But he certainly was also no devil. In fact, if any comparison applies, it may well be one drawn from antiquity, namely, that of Cincinnatus, who saved the Roman Republic by temporarily becoming its dictator. Like Cincinnatus, General Pinochet voluntarily relinquished his dictatorship. He did so after both preventing a Communist takeover and imposing major pro-free-market reforms, inspired largely by Milton Friedman (who in large part was himself inspired by Ludwig von Mises [a prominent economist, considered one of the leaders of the "Austrian School" approach]). The effect of these reforms was to make Chile's the most prosperous and rapidly progressing economy in Latin America. Thereafter, in the words of his *New York Times'* "largely hostile" obituary, he used his remaining power to "set limits, for example, on economic policy debates with frequent warnings that he would not tolerate a return to statist measures."

General Pinochet was thus one of the most extraordinary dictators in history, a dictator who stood for major limits on the power of the state, who imposed such limits, and who sought to maintain such limits after voluntarily giving up his dictatorship.

When General Pinochet stepped down, he did so with a guarantee of immunity from prosecution for his actions while in power. However, the present and previous regime in Chile violated this agreement and sought to ensnare the General in a web of legal actions and law suits, making the last years of his life a period of turmoil. This was a clear violation of contract, comparable to the seizure of property in violation of contract. Not surprisingly the regimes in question were avowedly socialist. As a result of their breach, it is now considerably less likely that the world will soon see any other dictator voluntarily relinquish his power. The Chilean socialists will have taught him that to be secure, he must remain in power until he dies.

Pinochet's Successes Do Not Justify Dictatorship

Dictatorship, like war, is always an evil. Like war, it can be justified only when it is necessary to prevent a far greater evil, namely, as in this case, the imposition of the far more comprehensive and severe, permanent totalitarian dictatorship of the Communists.

Despite the fact that General Pinochet was able to use his powers as dictator to enact major pro-free-market reforms, dictatorship should never be seen as justified merely as a means of instituting such reforms, however necessary and desirable they may be. Dictatorship is the most dangerous of political institutions and easily produces catastrophic results. This is because a dictator is not restrained by any need for public discussion and debate and thus can easily leap headlong into disasters that would have been avoided had there been the freedom to criticize his proposed actions and to oppose them. And even when his policies may be right, the fact that they are imposed in defiance of public opinion operates greatly to add to their unpopularity and thus to make permanent change all the more difficult.

Leftist peasants stand guard outside a farm they have seized in southern Chile in December 1970. Signs in Spanish read: "We demand land for those who work it. Bread, land, socialism. We shall triumph." © AP Images.

On the basis of such considerations, when asked many years ago what he would do if he were appointed dictator, von Mises replied, "I would resign". . . .

The Fable of Benign Socialism

Some of the responses to my [thoughts] on General Pinochet have reminded me that along with the fable of Santa Claus and his reindeer, which is so prominent right now because it is the Christmas Season, there is another fable that is still going around. And while the Santa Claus fable is innocent, serving merely to entertain small children, this one is definitely not innocent, but positively vicious. *It is the fable that those who are responsible for the attempt to socialize a country's economic system, such as Chile's, are well-intentioned and therefore deserve to be immune from bodily harm and certainly do not deserve ever to be killed.*

According to this fable, in a country such as Chile under Allende, Marxist boys and girls are happily singing and dancing, their faces glowing with love of the downtrodden, while they attempt the joyous task of building a socialist economic system. To be sure, there are also dark forces at work in the fable: again and again, wherever the innocent and happy Marxists go and accomplish their work "Soviet Russia, Communist China, Cuba, and all the other various satellites" impoverishment, enslavement, and mass murder inexplicably always seen to follow.

Of course, according to the fable, this cannot have anything to do with the nature of socialism and the actions of the Marxists who establish it. It just happens. Equally inexplicably, unless it be simply because of their evil nature, mean, nasty men appear, who for no good reason lay hold of the innocent Marxists and beat and kill them, as did Pinochet's soldiers in Chile in response to the Marxists' attempt to socialize the economy of that country. What a horror, what an outrage against good and innocent Marxists! Such evil surely deserves to be severely punished!

End of fable.

Socialism Is Inherently Violent

I have made it part of my life's work to throw intellectual ice water in the faces of people who have allowed themselves to become so deluded as to accept such a fable. And here, straight from my book *Capitalism,* is a good-sized bucketful of that intellectual ice water:

> Let us begin by considering the means employed to achieve socialism. We observe two phenomena that are not unrelated. First, wherever socialism has actually been enacted, as in the Communist-bloc countries and Nazi Germany, violent and bloody means have been used to achieve it and/or maintain it. And, second, where socialist parties have come to power but abstained from wholesale violence and bloodshed, as in Great Britain, Israel, and Sweden, they have *not* enacted socialism, but retained a so-called mixed economy, which they did not radically or fundamentally alter. Let us consider the reasons for these facts.
>
> *Even if a socialist government were democratically elected, its first act in office in implementing socialism would have to be*

an act of enormous violence, namely, the forcible expropriation of the means of production. The democratic election of a socialist government would not change the fact that the seizure of property against the will of its owners is an act of force. A forcible expropriation of property based on a democratic vote is about as peaceful as a lynching based on a democratic vote. It is a cardinal violation of individual rights. The only way that socialism could truly come into existence by peaceful means would be if property owners voluntarily donated their property to the socialist state. But consider. If socialism had to wait for property owners to voluntarily donate their property to the state, it would almost certainly have to wait forever. If socialism is ever to exist, therefore, it can only come about by means of force force applied on a massive scale, against all private property.

Further, in the case of the socialization of the entire economic system, as opposed to that of an isolated industry, no form of compensation to the property owners is possible. In the case of an isolated nationalization, the government can largely compensate the former owners by taxing the rest of the property owners to some extent. If the government seizes all property, however, and simply abolishes private ownership, then there is just no possibility of compensation. The government simply steals everyone's property lock, stock, and barrel. In these circumstances, property owners will almost certainly resist and try to defend their rights by force if necessary, as they properly should.

This explains why it takes the Communists to achieve socialism, and why the Social Democrats always fail to achieve socialism. The Communists, in effect, know that they are out to steal all of men's property from them and that if they expect to succeed, they had better come armed and prepared to kill the property owners, who will attempt to defend their rights. The Social Democrats, on the other hand, are held back by fear from taking the steps that would be necessary to achieve socialism.

In sum, the essential facts are these. Socialism must commence with an enormous act of theft. Those who seriously

> want to steal must be prepared to kill those whom they plan to rob. In effect, the Social Democrats are mere con men and pickpockets, who engage in empty talk about pulling the "big job"—socialism—someday, and who flee before the first sign of resistance by their intended victims. The Communists, on the other hand, are serious about pulling the "big job." They are armed robbers prepared to commit murder. This is why the Communists are able to implement socialism. Of the two, only the Communists are willing to employ the bloody means that are necessary to implement socialism. . . .

The above analysis applies to Chile at the time of General Pinochet's coup. At that time, President Allende, despite having been elected with only 36 percent of the vote, was aggressively pressing ahead, as even the *New York Times'* largely hostile obituary admits, "with a Socialist program to nationalize mines, banks and strategic industries, split up large rural estates into communal farms, and impose price controls." (Not surprisingly, such measures, as the *Times* notes, "soon resulted in steep declines in production, shortages of consumer goods and explosive inflation."

Pinochet's Harsh Coup Was a Proportionate Response

The essential point here is that a massive armed robbery on the part of the Marxist Allende government was actually in progress. It possessed armed "militias" and was using them to seize people's property. According to the *Wall Street Journal's* obituary, the regime was also acting in clear defiance of the Chilean Supreme Court, which denounced it for "an open and willful contempt of judicial decisions" that created the threat of an "imminent breakdown of legality."

So long as Marxists are content merely to write, speak, and otherwise fantasize about the destruction of capitalism and the establishment of socialism, they have every right to be left alone, just as every one else has who harms no one but himself. But when they begin to act out their fantasy in the real world and commit armed robbery, which, as I have shown, is the only means of achieving their goal, then they forfeit their rights, including their right to life.

The right to life, liberty, and property, which every man possesses, carries with it the right to self-defense. Exercise of the right of self-defense includes killing those who are an imminent threat to one's life. It includes killing those who are an imminent threat to one's life in one's attempt to defend one's property, which is what armed robbers always are, Marxist or otherwise. If the Marxists killed or beaten in Chile had wanted to avoid such treatment, they should have stayed home, written another book or article, given another lecture or speech, or gone to another protest meeting or rally. They should not have set out to steal other people's property.

The Allende Government Was Too Dangerous

True enough, all the writing, speaking, and peaceful protest in the world have no prospect of ever achieving socialism, because they will never persuade very many people to voluntarily donate their property to a socialist state. So at bottom, it must all be futile, unless at some point it erupts into violent action.

The implication of this is that unless Marxists can be satisfied, as the Social Democrats have apparently learned to be, with merely partial and largely token movement toward their goal, such as provided by the establishment and expansion of the welfare state, they are doomed to permanent frustration. At the same time, those of them who continue to be committed to the actual achievement of their goal of socialism, cannot be expected to tolerate such frustration permanently. At some point, it would seem, almost inevitably, they must erupt into violent action, because that is the only path that can ever achieve their goal.

Such Marxists, such socialists, i.e., the serious, dedicated ones, are not at all saints or martyrs, but dangerous people with a criminal mentality.

Viewpoint 4

What Pinochet Did for Chile

Robert A. Packenham and William Ratliff

In the following viewpoint, the authors focus on the lasting legacy of Augusto Pinochet's social and economic programs. Although the harshness of his military tactics were obviously regrettable, they argue that many of Pinochet's policies—especially his economic policies—have withstood the test of time, proven to be well-balanced and robust, and are now emulated throughout the developed and developing world. William Ratliff is the curator of the Americas collection at Stanford University's Hoover Institution, where he specializes in Latin American and US foreign policy. He is editor of the periodicals Yearbook on International Communist Affairs *and* Journal of Interamerican Studies. *Robert A. Packenham is professor emeritus of political science at Stanford University and the author of* Liberal America and the Third World *and* The Dependency Movement.

The late strongman ruled harshly but left behind the most successful country in Latin America. By Robert A. Packenham and William Ratliff.

Robert A. Packenham and William Ratliff, "What Pinochet Did for Chile," *Hoover Digest*, no. 1, 2007.

Chile's former president, General Augusto Pinochet, died in December. Some of his legacies are well known, but others are not.

Pinochet directed the coup of September 11, 1973, and presided until 1990 over a military regime that violated human rights, shut down political parties, canceled elections, constrained the press and trade unions, and engaged in other undemocratic actions during its more than 16 years of rule. These facts are important and widely recounted.

A number of other important truths about the Pinochet period and its legacy are equally well documented but less well known. Indeed, they are often not acknowledged at all. (A notable partial exception to this rule was the *Washington Post* editorial of December 12 [2006] that bore the headline "A dictator's double standard: Augusto Pinochet tortured and murdered. His legacy is Latin America's most successful country.") We will focus on the generally neglected, discounted, distorted, and sometimes falsely denied or suppressed aspects of the Pinochet legacy that have truly made Chile, despite its continuing challenges, "Latin America's most successful country."

What Kind of Democracy Did the Coup Displace?

The 1973 coup is often represented as having destroyed Chilean democracy. Such characterizations are half-truths at best. In the late 1960s and early 1970s, Chile's democracy was already well on the road to self-destruction. The historian James Whelan caught its tragic essence when he wrote that Chile's was a "cannibalistic democracy, consuming itself." Eduardo Frei Montalva, Chile's president from 1964 to 1970, who helped to bring in Salvador Allende as his successor, later called the latter's presidency "this carnival of madness." Freedoms increasingly overwhelmed responsibilities. Lawlessness became rampant. Uncontrolled leftist violence had also been escalating during the government of Christian Democrat Frei Montalva, before Allende became president and long before Pinochet played any role whatsoever in Chilean politics.

In 1970, Allende won 36.2 percent of the popular vote, less than the 38.6 percent he had taken in 1964 and only 1.3 percent more than the runner-up. According to the constitution, the legislature could have given the presidency to either of the top two candidates. It chose Allende only after he pledged explicitly to abide by the constitution. "A few months later," Whelan reports, "Allende told fellow leftist Regis Debray that he never actually intended to abide by those commitments but signed just to finally become president." In legislative and other elections over the next three years, Allende and his Popular Unity (UP) coalition, dominated by the Communist and Socialist parties, never won a majority, much less a mandate, in any election. Still Allende tried to "transition" (his term) Chile into a Marxist-Leninist economic, social, and political system.

Allende's closest UP allies were the Communists, the right wing of the UP, but both were pressed to move faster than they wanted by the left wing of the UP, mainly members of Allende's Socialist Party, and by ultraleftists (the term used by the Communists) to the left of the UP. Violence escalated rapidly, with the extreme left, including many members of the president's own party, seizing properties and setting up independent zones in cities and the countryside, often contrary to what Allende and the Communists thought prudent. In the process Allende, his supporters, and extremists they could not control virtually destroyed the economy, fractured the society, politicized the military and the educational systems, and rode roughshod over Chilean constitutional, legal, political, and cultural traditions. Thus by July 1973, if not earlier, Chile was looking at an incipient civil war.

Many on the left had long believed that capitalism and democracy were incompatible. In a brazen demonstration of its contempt for majority wishes, and for the institutions of what it called "bourgeois democracy," the pro-Allende newspaper *Puro Chile* reported the results of the March 1973 legislative elections with this headline: "The People, 43%. The Mummies, 55%."

During his visit to Cuba in 1972, Augusto Pinochet (right) waves from a balcony accompanied by Cuban dictator Fidel Castro. © Romano Cagnoni/Getty Images.

This attitude and the actions that followed from it galvanized the center-left and right, whose candidates had received almost two-thirds of the votes in the 1970 election, against Allende. On August 22, 1973, the Chamber of Deputies, whose members had been elected just five months earlier, voted 81–47 that Allende's regime had systematically "destroyed essential elements of institutionality and of the state of law." (The Supreme Court had earlier condemned the Allende government's repeated violations of court orders and judicial procedures.) Less than three weeks later, the military, led by newly appointed army commander in chief Pinochet, overthrew the government. The coup was supported by Allende's presidential predecessor, Eduardo Frei Montalva; by Patricio Aylwin, the first democratically elected president after democracy was restored in 1990; and by an overwhelming majority of the Chilean people. Cuba and the United States were actively involved on opposite sides, but the main players were always Chilean.

Authoritarian, Not Totalitarian

The Chilean military regime from 1973 to 1990 was authoritarian, certainly, but not totalitarian. This distinction is fundamental in comparative political analysis. Totalitarian regimes legitimize and practice very high degrees of penetration into all aspects of the economy, society, religion, culture, and family, whereas authoritarian regimes do not. Totalitarian regimes have dominant single parties; coherent, highly articulated, widely disseminated ideologies; very high levels of mass mobilization and participation directed and manipulated by the regime; and a strict control over candidates, when there are any, and policies. Authoritarian regimes have mentalities more than ideologies, low levels of political participation, and limited pluralism and competition of policies and political actors (including the press), with some constraints on regime control and manipulation of the polity, society, economy, family, religion, culture, and the press.

Consider also the two types of regimes' different propensities to enable a transition to democracy. Totalitarian systems—once in place and short of external military conquest and occupation—are much harder to change than authoritarian ones. Pinochet's authoritarianism in Chile ended after 16 years in a peaceful and constitutional transfer of power, permitted by a constitution passed in 1980; Castro's totalitarian regime in Cuba has lasted 48 years so far. Chile's democracy after 1990 has been vigorous and stable. As reported by Hector Schamis in the *Journal of Democracy* (October 2006), Chile's current foreign minister, Alejandro Foxley, recognized early in the first post-Pinochet democratic government that "the constitutional rules left by Pinochet had 'somewhat ironically fostered a more democratic system,' for they forced major actors into compromise rather than confrontation and, by 'avoiding populism,' increased 'economic governability.'"

The Economic Legacy

It has become fashionable in some quarters lately to claim that Chile's successful record of economic development in recent decades actually began in 1990, during the first civilian government since 1973. That claim is false. The historical record is clear. President Pinochet and his civilian advisers, after an elaborate and lengthy process of deliberation and decision making in 1973–1975, in which various alternative courses of action were considered, put in place the radically new set of market-oriented structures and policies that have been and remain the foundations of Chile's subsequent three decades of economic and social development. This new model, which we call social capitalism, was adjusted, revised, and supplemented during the Pinochet years, most importantly in response to an economic crisis in the early 1980s and also in the post-1990 civilian years. But its main elements have not changed, and thus far no post-1990 government has proposed or seriously considered going back to either of the two previous, failed models, namely, state capitalism (1938–70) or state socialism (1970–73).

As the then finance minister, Alejandro Foxley, said in a 1991 interview: "We may not like the government that came before us. But they did many things right. We have inherited an economy that is an asset." All four civilian governments since 1990 have maintained the new, more market-oriented economic and social models inherited from the military regime. Although there were changes at the margins after 1990, the point of sharpest and deepest positive change was unquestionably 1973 and immediately thereafter, not 1970 or 1990.

The Neoliberalism Myth

It is often said and widely believed that Pinochet's economic reforms eliminated any significant role of the state in the economy. The claim is that he introduced a neoliberal model, that is, raw, savage capitalism of the kind attributed to Chile in the nineteenth century. The facts are otherwise. Chile's largest industry and biggest foreign-exchange earner by far is copper, which was nationalized in the late 1960s and early 1970s *and has remained so ever since*. Domestic banks were deregulated in the late 1970s but reregulated with vigor in the early 1980s. Poverty had increased enormously during and in the wake of the UP's disastrous economic policies, and it decreased only as a result of the state-led stabilization policies, structural reforms, and targeted social programs of the Pinochet period. Major state expenditures for direct action social programs targeted to the poorest of the poor were initiated in the middle 1980s, not after 1990. Poverty levels, as high as 50 percent in 1984, were reduced to 34 percent by 1989. They continued to fall after 1990 to 15 percent in 2005. The Concertación, the alliance of political parties of the center and left that has won the past four presidential elections, deserves some credit for the post-1990 years, but so does the Pinochet government. It created the underlying economic policies and structures in the 1970s and 1980s that the Concertación maintained and that produced jobs for the poor and an economic surplus to enable targeted state antipoverty programs.

Legacies for the World

The innovations in economic and social policy of the Pinochet government had significant influences on, and implications for, not only subsequent governments in Chile but also the rest of Latin America and the wider world. Today almost the entire globe relies on the state less and on markets more than in 1973. The first country in the world to make that momentous break with the past—away from socialism and extreme state capitalism toward more market-oriented structures and policies—was not Deng Xiaoping's China or Margaret Thatcher's Britain in the late 1970s, Ronald Reagan's United States in 1981, or any other country in Latin America or elsewhere. It was Pinochet's Chile in 1975.

At that time the Chilean economic model was considered anathema almost everywhere—partly because of its association with Chile's military regime but also because it was viewed (wrongly, as it turned out) as an unthinkable, reactionary model per se, especially for developing countries. (Of the many military regimes in Latin America in the sixties, seventies, and eighties, the only one to break with state capitalism was Chile's.) But global perceptions of the Chilean economic model changed, slowly at first, more rapidly and massively after the mid-1980s. By now, the economic policies of most countries of Latin America; North America; Western, Central, and Eastern Europe; China; India; Russia and its former republics; much of Africa; and many other places around the world have followed the Chilean lead rather than fled from it.

The Autumn of Two Dictators

Pinochet's death occurred just as Fidel Castro was lying gravely ill in Cuba. Have commentators described and evaluated them with equal accuracy and fairness over the decades?

Castro killed at least as many Cubans as Pinochet did Chileans. Pinochet's government has been justly condemned for engaging in some terrorist activities abroad, from Argentina to the United States. Amnesty International strongly supported the Chilean leader's extradition to Spain in 1998 for a trial it thought would enact justice. But Castro trained thousands of guerrillas from countries all over the world and sent hundreds of thousands of Cuban troops to many countries on at least three continents to launch and wage wars that brought untold death and destruction. We can't recall human rights organizations agitating for his extradition, or for his being brought to justice even posthumously in Cuba. Finally, Chile is the most successful case of economic, social, and political development in Latin America and a pioneer in the global shift to enlightened social capitalism. Cuba is a dismal, impoverished, dynastic totalitarian anachronism.

How many nations a decade or century from now will aspire to the "successes" of Fidel Castro—or of Salvador Allende? A much more positive case can be made for major parts of Pinochet's legacy. It's time to acknowledge that the legacies of the Pinochet years are a much better mix than they are usually said to be.

Viewpoint 5

Pinochet Was Not Responsible for the "Chilean Miracle"

Heraldo Muñoz

In the following viewpoint, the author argues that there was no "Chilean Miracle" under Pinochet. He writes that Chile's economic modernization had its roots in the 1920s, and even Pinochet's expansion of agricultural exports during his rule were only possible because of land reforms put in place by the leftist governments of the 1960s and 1970s. The bulk of Chile's robust economic growth only took hold after a series of moves in the 1990s following Pinochet leaving office. These new policies made Chile's economy more stable by reducing reliance on unregulated markets, which is contrary to the "Chicago School" economic theories that had guided Pinochet, the viewpoint argues. Heraldo Muñoz is a Chilean politician who cofounded the ultimately successful campaign to vote Augusto Pinochet out of office in the 1988 Chilean free elections. Muñoz served as Chile's ambassador to the United Nations from 2003 to 2010 and has written several books including The Dictator's Shadow: Life Under Augusto Pinochet.

The main problem for Pinochet's apologists was the brutality and corruption of their man. If only Pinochet had modernized Chile's economy to make it a model for the developing world without killing and torturing his opponents and getting caught with his hands in the cookie jar. Conservatives still feel obliged to defend the man and the regime that gave many of them access to riches and prosperity. The bottom line for Pinochet supporters is that, despite his sins, "he made the trains run on time," as Mussolini used to be praised.

They're not completely wrong. Chile's economic mentality changed under Pinochet. Economic policies that seemed bold at the time proved innovating and were incorporated in the policy mix by democratic governments, lending stability to the economy. A broad spectrum of players came to accept the idea that Chile needed to continue growing, and that private initiatives ought to be stimulated. Fiscal rigor and sound macroeconomic policies were a capital that did not belong exclusively to Pinochet, though he had given the green light to his economists to put those policies into practice. But it wasn't Pinochet's doing alone. The groundwork for Pinochet's economic modernization was laid by his predecessors. Land reform of the 1960s and early '70s broke up the inefficient semifeudal estates, allowing the military regime to stimulate the creation of agroindustry as a base for an export-driven economy. Chile's modernization really began around 1920 and had nothing to do with the Chicago Boys. By the time of the coup in 1973, thanks to the efforts of many previous governments, Chileans enjoyed a high level of education (illiteracy was less than 10 percent by 1970), and malnutrition and infant mortality had been declining for decades. Chilean universities were among the best in the Americas; there was an efficient transportation infrastructure; the Central Bank, the Internal Revenue Service, and the General Comptroller's Office, among others, were all solid state institutions. Chile's accumulated sociocultural capital were prerequisites for the success of the Pinochet government's economic reforms.

Pinochet's Extreme Measures Were Needless

The key question is this: Was Pinochet necessary? Was the price paid for economic change under Pinochet worth it? Clearly it was not. To begin, systematic repression and violence against dissidents was not inevitable. Very likely, the economic reforms of the Pinochet regime would have been sternly opposed in a democratic context by labor unions, members of Congress, and political parties; but their implementation, even under authoritarian rule, did not require the murder of union leaders, the exile of thousands of dissidents, the torture and disappearance of political prisoners, the terrorist bombing of exiled leaders, and a permanent state of internal war. [Nobel Prize-Winning Peruvian author] Mario Vargas Llosa has asserted that a Pinochet-type regime is not a necessary evil; no nation "needs to pass through dictatorship to modernize and reach well-being." Reforms imposed by a dictatorship "always have a price in atrocities and civic and ethical sequels that are infinitely costlier than [the] status quo." Besides, without freedom and the rule of law, public opinion may not be willing to accept the sacrifices required for economic reform to succeed and endure. In the end, economic liberty seldom thrives in the absence of political freedom.

Could Chile have reached its present level of prosperity without Pinochet? My answer is yes. Many Latin American countries that endured economic crises in the 1970s and '80s, such as Brazil and Peru, eventually chose to introduce tough economic reforms—not without vigorous opposition to them. Even Colombia, confronting domestic war, was able to implement economic reforms in a reasonably democratic context.

The Actual Economic Miracle in Chile

Moreover, the social costs of Pinochet's economic policies were huge. Pinochet did not build a single hospital in all his years of power and the country's infrastructure was left practically untouched until the return of democracy. In 1970, 20 percent of

Chile's economic vitality can be seen in the bustling port city of Valparaiso. Many argue that the country's dramatic economic growth since the 1990s is the result of the policies of the democratic government that followed Pinochet's rule. © Mike Finn-Kelcey/age fotostock/Alamy.

Chile's population had lived under the poverty line; by 1990, when Pinochet left office, the poor had doubled to 40 percent. Average salaries during the Pinochet years were lower than in 1970. The real Chilean economic miracle truly occurred during the sixteen years following the return of democracy, when the economy grew 5.6 percent, almost doubling the growth rates of the previous three decades. Chile is the Latin American country that grew the most from 1990 to 2006. The country's GDP, at purchasing-power parity, is now well above those of Argentina, Brazil, and Mexico. Between 1985 and 2005, Chile's GDP per capita rose from 24 to 40 percent of U.S. levels, a noticeable exception in comparison to the region's overall record of relative decline. Poverty fell from nearly 40 percent of the population in 1990 to 13.7 percent in 2006. Meat consumption increased from 36.6 kilos per capita annually in 1990 to 79 kilos in 2006. The percentage of Chilean homes owning refrigerators and washing machines jumped from 55 and 37 percent, respectively, in 1992, to 96 and 94 percent in 2006. In short, it took the return to democracy in 1990 to bestow legitimacy on Pinochet's reforms and to expand and improve the country's economic and social record.

Pinochet's Legacy

Yet for many conservatives, and those who quietly profited under the dictator's rule, Pinochet remained a patriot who saved his country from Communism. Chile was surely polarized in 1973, and radical sectors within Allende's coalition, including my own Socialist Party, contributed to the climate of confrontation and insecurity. But the menace of leftist armed insurrection and the likelihood of imminent Communist takeover were highly exaggerated. The rapidity with which the perpetrators of the coup seized and held control of the country gainsays those myths. The violence that Pinochet unleashed was not a desperate expedient to save an imperiled country; it was a brutal power grab by what became a despotic regime.

GROSS DOMESTIC PRODUCT PER CAPITA IN CHILE AND LATIN AMERICA, 1950–2010

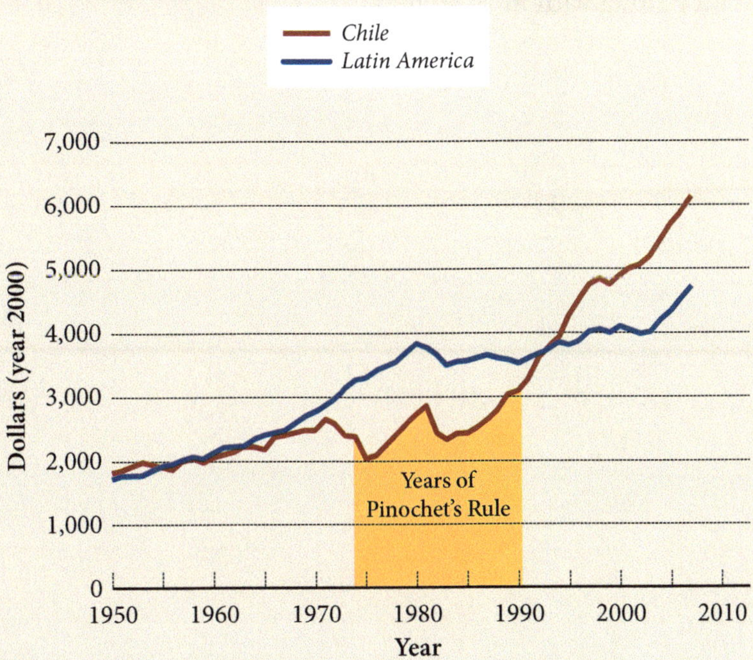

GDP calculated using constant year 2000 US dollars. Data compiled from the International Monetary Fund's World Economic Outlook Database and the United Nation's Economic Commission for Latin America. Data includes Argentina, Bolivia, Brazil, Chile, Colombia, Costa Rica, Dominican Republic, Ecuador, El Salvador, Guatemala, Haiti, Honduras, Mexico, Nicaragua, Panama, Paraguay, Peru, Uruguay, and Venezuela. Does not include Cuba due to missing data.

Source: Cantus and Solap, "Gross Domestic Product Per Capita at Constant Market Prices," *Wikipedia*, February 22, 2010.

Pinochet delivered order after a period of domestic instability and chaos, all of it exacerbated by the Nixon administration's covert and illegal efforts to remove President Allende. Allende was about to announce a plebiscite to resolve the nation's political impasse when the coup began; no matter how he would have fared in such an emergency referendum, his coalition had only the slimmest of chances of winning the 1976 presidential contest.

Many of those who favored the coup wanted the armed forces to simply restore order and then immediately call for elections. But having seized power, Pinochet decided to keep it, eliminating democracy along with its defenders.

VIEWPOINT 6

The Chilean Government's Attempts at Reparations Have Been Weak and Ineffectual

Roberta Bacic and Elizabeth Stanley

In the following viewpoint, the authors argue that although Chile's national efforts to confront the crimes of the Pinochet years have been laudable, they have been far from complete. The authors specifically criticize these efforts for failing to publicly expose torturers, adequately compensate victims, foster a meaningful and open dialogue about the past, or challenge the conspiracy of silence surrounding government-sponsored torture in Chile. Roberta Bacic is a Chilean-born writer and human rights researcher. Elizabeth Stanley teaches at the School of Social and Cultural Studies at the Victoria University of Wellington in New Zealand.

Until the establishment of the *Comisión Nacional Sobre Prisión Politica y Tortura* (National Commission for Political Imprisonment and Torture, hereafter the *Comisión*), the issues of political imprisonment and torture had been neglected in Chile. This is not to say that there has been no movement at all on the issue. In 1991, the Rettig Report acknowledged torture as a recurrent and institutionalised event, and torture was shown to have preceded most of the executions and 'disappearances' of

Roberta Bacic and Elizabeth Stanley, "Dealing with Torture in Chile Achievements and Shortcomings of the 'Valech Report'," *NMRZ*, June 3, 2005.

victims. Further, in the transition from dictatorship, some torture survivors have been able to receive personal medical assistance from the Government, others were able to regain their civil rights by challenging official documentation that presented them as criminals, while some have been accepted as viable witnesses in human rights court cases. However, these rights were hard to attain and, at an official level, those who survived imprisonment and torture were not generally acknowledged.

The *Comisión* was established on 12 August 2003 by Chilean President Ricardo Lagos. Operating under the banner 'There is no Tomorrow without Yesterday', the eight Commissioners published their findings in November 2004. The full Report, spanning 638 pages, is only available on the internet and has not been made widely available in printed form.

Testimony Shows That a High Percentage of Political Detainees Were Tortured

Despite the short time-frame to collate stories, thousands of survivors contacted the *Comisión* to relay their testimonies. Indeed, 35,868 individuals approached the *Comisión* and its representatives in just 6 months and in Santiago, the *Comisión* met between 114 and 240 people each day. Most people gave their testimony in Chile (37% in Santiago and 54% in other Chilean regions) however 9% of statements were given across 40 different countries. Such a response indicates the real need that many victims had to have their experiences officially acknowledged.

The *Comisión* details that there were 1,132 detention centres across Chile. Victims were tortured in police stations, military installations, schools and hospitals, among other sites. Torture was state policy and commonplace for political detainees, indeed the Report found that 94% of all political detainees were tortured. In line with the *Comisión's* mandate, 33,221 individuals were proven to have been detained; these victims had spent an average of 180.1 days in prison. Out of this group, 27,255 people were officially registered as victims of torture. Approximately

Findings of Chile's National Commission for Political Imprisonment and Torture

- Chile had 1,132 detention centers.
- 33,221 individuals were proven to have been detained.
- Victims spent an average of 180.1 days in prison.
- 27,255 people were officially registered as victims of torture.
- 94% of all political detainees were tortured.
- 87.5% of victims were men; 12.5% were female.
- A third of all victims faced electric shock torture.
- Nearly all female victims reported that they had suffered sexual torture.

Roberta Bacic and Elizabeth Stanley, "Dealing with Torture in Chile: Achievements and Shortcomings of the 'Valech Report,'" Nürnberger Menschenrechtszentrum (Nuremberg Human Rights Center), June 3, 2005. www.menschenrechte.org.

19% (6,845) of the individuals who approached the *Comisión* were not accepted as victims and are not listed in the Report.

Of those who were officially designated as victims of torture, the following statistics can be provided:

The worst period of torture occurred immediately after the coup, as more than 18,000 (67.4%) people were tortured between September and December 1973. Another 5,266 (19.32%) people were tortured between January 1974 and August 1977 and the remaining 3,625 (13.3%) victims suffered torture between August 1977 and March 1990.

The majority (87.5%) of victims were men, as women represented 12.5% of victims. A third of all victims faced electric shock torture and nearly all female victims reported that they has suffered sexual torture. The majority (27,153) were adults during detention however 102 children were also registered as victims, these children were either born during imprisonment or detained with their parents.

At the time of detention: 4% of victims were under 18; 9.7% were between 18 and 20; 44.2% were between 21 and 30 years old; 25.4% were between 31 and 40 years old; 12.5% were between 41 and 50; and. 4.3% were over 50. Most of the young adults belonged to political parties and acknowledged that they had also been trade union members. Of those victims who were under 18 years of age, 766 were between 16 and 17, 226 were 13 to 15 and 88 were 12 or less. None of these children were legally responsible at the time of their detention.

At the time of reporting, the *Comisión* states that 9% of victims have died (their testimony was presented by their next of kin) and that 83% of the victims are over 51 years. 27% of victims are retired or unemployed; as such, these individuals tend to be in vulnerable financial situations.

A Rigorous Investigative Process

The mandate of the *Comisión* restricted cases to those who were detained and could prove that their detention was politically motivated. Generally, this was focused on cases where individuals could prove that they had been detained without due process, or that they were arrested under one of the special decrees created by the regime, or that they had been arrested by the DINA (the secret service body), or that they had been arrested on accusations of a regime-established crime (eg. being a member of a political party). Those presenting to the *Cómisión* had to demonstrate that the regime had violated their rights as constituted by international and national law. Those giving testimony, as either a survivor or a surviving relative, had to therefore prove the political basis of the detention.

While each testimony followed a set form, so that each individual would comply with certain standards of required information, all had to be accompanied by documentation that established the nature of the individual's detention. Evidence was based on witness testimony, detention centre records as well as other documentation from state agencies, human rights organizations, contemporary media accounts, international bodies and the armed forces.

Thus, the *Comisión* did not take an investigatory approach to its work. Indeed, interested parties—such as victims' associations, human rights experts, religious and moral leaders—had to request meetings with the *Comisión* if they wanted their voices to be heard. This working approach, that 'sorts out the problem by leaving out the people' who have been affected by and have worked on the topic for years would seem to run against 'much of the writing on societies emerging from a period of political violence has stressed that all the different voices must be listened to, if we seek to deal seriously and responsibly with the past'.

A Strong Public Desire for Justice

The *Comisión* emerged thirteen years after the Rettig Commission. While we may never fully know the reasons why the *Comisión* was implemented, we can identify recent events that have contributed to a new space in which violations could be addressed.

For instance, it would seem consistent that the *Comisión* would occur after the torture charges brought against General Pinochet in Europe [in 1999]. During Pinochet's detention in London, the Chilean government argued that the issue of human rights was one to be dealt with at the national, not the international, level. Following his release, a sequence of events has developed in the human rights arena. For example, Pinochet's immunity has been challenged and Judge Guzmán has continued the case against him in the Chilean courts.

Simultaneously, other cases have developed and these have resulted in the conviction of many significant dictatorship figures. For example, Pinochet's former Head of intelligence,

Manuel Contreras, together with hundreds of former military and police officers have been prosecuted for their involvement in human rights violations during the first five years of the dictatorship and been held at Punta Peuco, a privileged prison constructed for the purpose of detaining human rights violators. In 2003, a Florida civil court also held that a Chilean former army officer. Armando Fernández Larios, was liable for the torture and killing of Winston Cabello, an economist. Fernández was ordered to pay $4 million in damages.

More recently, a 2005 US Senate report indicated that Pinochet controlled 128 bank accounts in the United States. Using aliases to open accounts, it is thought that he held over $19 million of undeclared 'revenue'. While such reports act as an international denouncement of Pinochet's corrupt affairs, Chilean groups have also sought to shame human rights violators in their local environment. The well known campaign group 'Funa', for instance, names individuals as abusers in public. This group has consistently exposed the lack of justice and accountability for human rights violations in Chile.

With such events the Chilean government has encountered a new, safer space to pursue accountability. At the start of the new century, human rights perpetrators have held less sway in Chilean politics and law. Moreover, Chile has been keen to maintain its international image and status as a country that has dealt well with its past.

The *Comisión* was constructed in this context. However, even the Commissioners themselves raised the question of the meaning of writing a report thirty years after events occurred. As they note:

> After having listened to intimate, whispered narratives, told with pain and even with tears, and after seeing the physical and psychological evidence, as well as the family and social damage—some of which can not be repaired or restituted—of so many Chileans imprisoned and tortured we have no doubt

> that we had to complete this part of the truth, as well as possible, for the reparation and justice that the country owes to its brothers and sisters, and to progress along the roads of the always difficult and necessary encounter and reconciliation among Chileans.

For the Commissioners, the Report emerged from the continued national need to deal with the long-standing issues of truth, reparation, justice and reconciliation. . . .

An Incomplete Attitude Toward Openness and Accountability

The impact of the official acknowledgement of the extensive use of torture during dictatorship cannot be denied. To view the extent of the lists of torture victims is overwhelming. However, on reflection, the list in itself cannot be the only manifestation of what happened and the decision that victims' testimonies cannot be disclosed for fifty years will ensure that the truth that is exposed is a partial one. While some torture survivors may have the ability to make public their suffering, most will not. This lack of exposure of detailed testimonies will mean that the Chilean population will not understand the diverse ways in which people endured detention and torture.

The truth of torture is also tested by the fact that lists detail the tortured but do not identify torturers. Those who suffered torture are the only ones who are exposed in this official truth-finding. This has resulted in sharp criticism of the Report. After all, in such a safe political situation, why has the *Comisión* continued to protect perpetrators? If an official body like this can not face truth as a whole, then who could? In response to these omissions, a counter-report has been established, by a group of ex-political prisoners in Santiago, to identify and castigate torturers as well as those who actively supported torture. Such actions represent an attempt to devalue the status of torturers within Chilean society—an action that should be undertaken by the government.

Given the lack of official recognition of torturers, perpetrators have also continued to disseminate messages and threats to the population. Some officials from the armed forces have claimed that torture was an aberration, only attributable to individual, unruly officers while others have refused to accept any institutional responsibility at all. For example, Rodolfo Stange and Fernando Cordero, high-ranking police officials, argued that they had no reason to argue for forgiveness. Cordero even went so far as to say that the ones who would have to ask for forgiveness were the ones who were responsible for events before 11 September 1973.

Finally, despite the vast number of individuals who have come forward to give their testimony, we must also be mindful that there are many others who did not. For instance, as far as we have been informed, in some countries only a few individuals gave their testimony to the Chilean Consulate while most individuals collectively agreed not to engage with the process. As far as these groups were concerned, government officials could not be trusted to effectively represent their needs. Fear and mistrust are still present in their lives.

Victims Have Been Poorly Compensated for Their Suffering

The *Comisión* itself has detailed that the damage inflicted against torture victims cannot be adequately repaired or restituted. As a symbolic gesture, each identified victim will receive an equal monthly payment of 112,000 pesos (US$190). This amount was not criticised by right-wing parties in Chile but by Gonzalo Martner, previous President of the Socialist party, who stated that 'the amount of payment should be differentiated according to what was endured'. Presently, the amount received by an individual who was held over several years is the same given to a victim detained for a week.

Reparations are not, however, confined to financial payment. The *Comisión* also provides for practical measures and the Report states that victims will receive health, education and housing benefits. Some of these services will provide welcome relief. However a question may be raised about access to education. Given the reality that most victims are over 50, this seems to be a benefit that can promote governmental good-will without too much cost.

The President's plea to victims to contribute their reparations to a special human rights fund, set up by the government also raises some consternation. The idea that a proposed National Human Rights Foundation might be funded by victims of torture, without asking perpetrating individuals and institutions to contribute to it, seems quite inappropriate. Let us remember that perpetrators have received well-paid salaries and pensions over the last 30 years while victims have had to wait to receive any symbolic reparation.

Little Justice for Torture Victims

As detailed above, a protective position for perpetrators and violating institutions has been set up. Perpetrators have not been named in the *Comisión* Report and the Chilean Congress approved a law, in Dec 2004, to ensure that testimonies cannot be revealed in court procedures over the next fifty years.

> It is clear, then, that the *Comisión* has not contributed in any way to the criminal prosecution of perpetrators. This has ensured that the equilibrium of power has been maintained in Chile, there has been no loss of prestige or status for perpetrators or violating institutions, and some individuals remain in powerful positions. With a recent Supreme Court decision to only allow judges six months to conclude human rights investigations and governmental announcements of a law to expedite human rights trials, opportunities for justice are being drastically curtailed. Such actions undermine the truth-finding of the Comisión.

Victims have a legal right to justice for the violations inflicted against them. Yet, without doubt, the actions of the *Comisión* as

Members of a Chilean Human Rights organization participate in a ceremony at Villa Grimaldi, a former detention and torture center, in Santiago, Chile, on September 10, 2013. © Martin Bernetti/AFP/Getty Images.

well as the Chilean government and courts in relation to the issue of accountability indicates that justice for torture will not be upheld within Chile.

With such activities exposed, the opportunities for reconciliation are hindered. The distance between victims and perpetrators together with the imbalance of power and the concessions given to perpetrators all contribute to a situation in which reconciliation can not be expected to happen. At previous reconciliation masses in Santiago, churches have been filled with military officials, politicians and judges while the relatives of the detained-disappeared have remained outside, not invited to participate. The same pattern appears to be repeated here. Those who were victimised, while publicly acknowledged, have not seen any devaluation of perpetrator's identity or status.

To engage in reconciliation, all individuals must have an awareness and understanding of different positions. This will be a difficult prospect for Chilean society if the *Comisión* does not publish its findings widely. The decision to expose the Report on the internet will mean that those who read the findings will inevitably be those who are already working in human rights, academics, those who gave testimony, and so on. The limitations of internet access will mean that many of those who represented themselves at the Comisión may not even get an opportunity to read the final Report. Moreover, those who do not want to read the findings, or do not know of its existence will continue not knowing.

Challenging the Conspiracy of Silence in Chile

In the Report, the Commissioners argued:

> It is important to point out that the results of the *Comisión* would not have been possible if we had not had the collaboration of thousands of victims, who in many cases finally decided to talk about their experiences, never before narrated. This allowed to end forever the conspiracy of silence that existed about torture for decades in our country.

As argued above, given the vast numbers of victims who did approach the *Comisión,* it is clear that many people did have a need to be officially acknowledged. Their previous silence does not demonstrate a lack of will to communicate on their part rather it represents a lack of will by Chilean society and government to actually listen to torture testimonies.

Yet, with this Report, the Commissioners propose that the silence of torture has ended. Given the limitations on the Report, discussed above, we would argue that Chilean society still has some way to go before it could affirm such a statement. The silence continues to exist for perpetrators and their supporters and victims' testimonies have been managed in such a way that speaking out about torture has been re-appropriated for political ends. We may acknowledge that over 35,000 approached the *Comisión* with testimonies of detention and torture. However, we still understand relatively little about the suffering those detained endured, how perpetrators legitimised their violations and the structures that allowed torture to flourish.

From such observations, there is a need for further, detailed work to be undertaken that addresses these concerns with those who approached the *Comisión*. In particular, it is imperative that we take the opportunity to examine survivors' understandings and experiences of the Comisión's work; to assess the personal and social repercussions of giving testimony in this way; and to address what survivors still require, in terms of truth, reparation, justice and reconciliation, to deal with their past. By asking such questions, the real value of the *Comisión's* work may be understood.

Chapter 3

Personal Narratives

Chapter Exercises

1. **Writing Prompt**

   Imagine you are a Chilean living under Augusto Pinochet's regime. Write a one-page journal entry about your daily life. Be sure to include the date and consider the difference between life for Chileans early and late in Pinochet's seventeen-year rule.

2. **Group Activity**

   Break into groups and compose five interview questions that would be useful if you were collecting oral histories from teens describing their experiences in Chile in 1973 and 1974. Remember that teenaged men were often forced to serve in Pinochet's military where they might be obliged to carry out brutal orders.

Viewpoint 1

An American Expatriate Observes the Coup from Within

Marc Cooper

Six months after President Salvador Allende's 1971 inauguration, the author of the following viewpoint was an idealistic twenty-six-year old who moved to Chile to experience what it was like to live under the world's first freely-elected Marxist leader. Ten months after arriving, Cooper was working for Allende, translating the president's speeches into English for broader publication. He was still serving as Allende's Spanish-English translator on September 11, 1973, when a violent military coup attacked the presidential palace, overthrew the elected socialist government, and installed General Augusto Pinochet as president. Marc Cooper is an American author, journalist, and journalism professor. The following viewpoint comes from his 2001 memoir, Pinochet and Me: A Chilean Anti-Memoir. *In it he recounts that chaotic period in Chile, his mounting nightmare as an American targeted by the new regime, and his inability to gain help from the US government, which supported the coup.*

Marc Cooper, *Pinochet and Me: A Chilean Anti-Memoir*. New York: Verso, 2001, pp. 30–53.

7 A.M., Tuesday September 11 . . .

I had gotten up early because my Chilean residency visa expired that day and I needed to renew it—an arduous process. For a year now I had been working as a translator to President Allende and, in this capacity, I was scheduled to travel with him the next week.

I knew that presidential translator status would afford me little advantage in navigating Chile's byzantine bureaucracy. Renewing my visa would still take the entire morning. And getting an Argentine visa so I could travel with Allende to Buenos Aires for the inauguration of the new Argentine president would take the rest of the day. An early start was imperative.

Taxis had become harder to come by as many of the cab companies had joined the work stoppage led by the Truckers' Association—a group floated with CIA dollars. Retail merchants, doctors, lawyers, almost everyone more elevated than manual workers and farmers had joined the stoppage. In daily entreaties, they pleaded openly with the armed forces to do away with the popularly elected Allende and restore Chile to Business-As-Usual.

Indeed, Chile had already pitched itself into a dizzying dance of chaos and blood. As Allende's reforms deepened, as he nationalized the American copper mines and telephone company, as large rural estates were handed over to their share-croppers, as wages soared and unions gained a voice in national affairs, as rents were lowered and taxes on the rich increased, the political Right and eventually the Centre jettisoned their attachment to the rule of law. Opposition groups fielded chain-swinging thugs against government marches. Oil pipelines were dynamited. Industrial production was sabotaged. The wealthy hoarded food and other consumer goods and then loudly protested the resulting shortages. . . .

The Right drew the noose tighter. Commerce and transport ground to a halt. The night before September 11, the transport stoppage had waylaid me and my girlfriend at Melvin's house. We had gone out as a foursome, wound up snacking at Melvin's, and got stranded without a way back to my downtown apartment.

My only chance of transport that morning was with my friends at Radio Taxi 33. Militant revolutionaries, the drivers there had long ago seized the company from its conservative owners and had turned the place into the most efficient cab service in Santiago. . . .

After a forty-five-minute wait on the corner, I became concerned. I went back to the house to call the taxi company again but, inexplicably, the phone lines were now permanently busy. I walked back to the corner and eventually was able to flag down a passing cab.

The driver, pale and harried, rolled down the window. "Can you take me downtown?" I asked.

"Downtown?"

"Yeah. To the immigration office," I answered.

With classic Chilean understatement and cool diplomacy the cabbie replied: "But, sir, there are problems downtown."

"Problems?"

"Yes, problems," he said refusing to be more specific. After all, these were highly polarized times. You never knew who you were talking to. One person's problem was another person's liberation. But a sinking feeling in my gut told me the worst was upon us.

Mustering my own diplomatic skills, I asked. "Problems, you say? Problems with men in uniform you mean?"

'Yes, sir, problems with men in uniform," the cabbie said. But now, the fear of the future already imprinted on him, he took what he probably knew would be his last foray into freedom for some time and added: "Yes, the f---ing fascists are overthrowing the government."

7:55 A.M., Tuesday September 11

Everyone else in the house was still asleep. I switched on the massive Grundig radio and waited impatiently for the vacuum tubes to warm up. As the audio came alive I turned the dial and confirmed the cabbie's report: virtually every station was playing the same military march.

I stopped the dial on Radio Corporación, the station of the Socialist Party. Allende was speaking, a nervous inflection in his voice. His words made material the nightmares that had haunted us for months: "This is the President of the Republic speaking from La Moneda Palace. Confirmed reports indicate that a sector of the Navy has isolated and occupied the port city of Valparaiso, which means an uprising against the government is under way . . . Under these circumstances, I call upon the workers of the country to occupy your workplaces . . . but I urge you to stay calm. At this moment, there have been no extraordinary troop movements in the capital . . . I am here defending the government that represents the will of the people . . ." Allende assured those listening that he would be back with any further information but that for the moment we should all remain in a state of alert.

On just about every other station on the dial a stern-voiced announcer suddenly materialized. By order of the military junta, he said, all radio stations were immediately to link up to the armed forces network or "they will be bombarded." The names of the four commanders making up the junta were then read: leading the National Police—the *carabineros*—was a general César Mendoza, a little-known name. For the Air Force there was Gustavo Leigh and for the Navy, Admiral José Merino. But the most important person on the list was Army General Augusto Pinochet. Pinochet, previously the Commander of the Santiago garrison, had two weeks earlier taken over as Commander-in-Chief, swearing his loyalty to the President he was now trying to overthrow.

Some more Prussian marches. And then another announcement. An ultimatum to President Allende. I sat chilled and shaking as I strained to scribble down the text of what a steely voice called Military Communiqué Number 2: "The Moneda Palace must be evacuated before 11am otherwise it will be attacked by the Chilean Air Force. The workers must remain in their workplaces and homes as it strictly prohibited to leave them. If they disobey, they will also be attacked by air and ground forces."

I sat paralyzed. A few moments later the same dry baritone voice read out Communiqué Number 3. Again I noted it on a yellow pad. "The population is hereby warned not to let themselves be carried away by incitements to violence from either foreign or national activists. And let the foreign ones know that in this country we do not accept violent attitudes or any extreme positions. This should be remembered as means are adopted for their rapid deportation from the country. Any resistance will be met with the full rigor of military justice."

Yet another announcement proclaimed a curfew "until further notice." Anyone found on the streets "will be shot on sight." I had roused the others in the house. We sat dumb-founded in the chilly living room listening to Radio Magallanes, the Communist Party station, boldly resisting the order to broadcast the armed forces network. Over the air, workers were being urged to report to their factories and organize defense committees.

But this was an empty gesture. Those of us who worked in the Allende government knew the sad truth: that in spite of the right-wing chorus that Allende had formed a "parallel army," we had no such units. Allende had been scrupulous in his commitment to a constitutional, legal, and peaceful transition to socialism. The only guns in the country, he vowed, would remain in the hands of the armed forces. Yes, some Socialists and others had formed clandestine militias—but they were operationally risible.

This war was going to be a short, one-sided massacre. And the tragic irony was that those conservative and centrist political forces that for 150 years had defended a constitutional system as long as it served their interests were now rebelling against it. The last man left standing in defense of the "bourgeois" constitution would be the Marxist President, AK-47 in hand.

10 A.M., Tuesday September 11

Miraculously, my first attempt to phone the office where I worked in the Moneda Palace went through. Over the sound of crackling gun fire, a secretary, Ximena, told me in tears that she and the others were about to flee the building. My next call was to the US Embassy—up on the fourteenth floor of an office building diagonally opposite the Moneda. I had had virtually no contact with the Embassy and had, in fact, made every effort to steer clear of it. Even my mail was routed to the Canadian Embassy—a government that had showed more sympathy to Allende.

But I phoned the US Embassy that morning hoping that some safety provisions were being made for resident Americans. I figured it was only a matter of hours before I would be swept up in the military dragnet.

The Embassy phone answered on the first ring. An accented English told me I was speaking with a Chilean employee—always more American than the Americans. When I asked if the Embassy had issued any special instructions, my respondent only laughed. "No special orders. Just stay off the streets." And then with another chuckle she added: "I'm looking out the window now with binoculars. Looks like Mr. Allende is finally going to get it." She hung up. . . .

4 P.M., Tuesday September 11

A non-stop cascade of military communiqués: that the Moneda had been bombed, that the Allende government was no longer, that all political activity was banned, that a dawn-to-dusk curfew was in effect, that the citizenry should denounce all "suspicious foreigners." As that first evening under military rule enveloped us I felt as if I were already in prison.

I knew I was a prime target: Allende's translator, an activist in the radical wing of the Socialist Party and a foreigner to boot at a moment when *all* foreigners were *ipso facto* suspect. I thought of my own apartment and cringed, a downtown high rise located directly across the street—no more than twenty yards—from the new junta headquarters. Régis Debray, the French writer and radical who had spent time with Che Guevara in Bolivia, had lived in my building when Allende first came to power. Other units were rented to exiled guerrillas from Argentina and Uruguay. The building teemed with the international New Left. One room of my apartment was stocked with the cheap editions of political classics and classic fiction made available under Allende. On my studio desk were copies of the work I had translated for Allende. In my top drawer was my passport, a visa to Cuba where I was scheduled to visit with Allende, and to top it all off, a .22 revolver with a couple of boxes of ammunition. On the floor were two radio transceivers that I was repairing for my buddies at RadioTaxi 33. In short, once the troops broke into my apartment, as they undoubtedly would, a warrant would be issued for a twenty-two-year-old American named Marc Cooper.

10 A.M., Friday September 14 . . .

I am embarrassed now, years later, to confess that I thought that, given the mounting bloodshed in Chile, the American Embassy on that day would be sending out rescue cars to pick up beleaguered stragglers like myself. I was under no illusions as to where the Embassy was at politically. The Nixon-Kissinger regime had made clear its intention to do away with Allende and it was now three days deep into implementing that goal. But I was deluded enough to think that, in order to avoid the uncomfortable spectacle of American citizens being killed by its new client military dictatorship, the US government might do something to protect us. In this I was entirely wrong.

As the curfew temporarily lifted that Friday I called the US Consulate. Explaining merely that I was an "American student," that I had done nothing wrong, but that the Chilean Police had raided my apartment and seized my passport, I told the Vice-Consul, Mrs. Tipton, I needed help. Even as I asked, my heart began to sink. Her husband was the Embassy's top "political officer," tied to the darkest aspects of US policy.

La Moneda, the presidential palace in Santiago, Chile, is bombarded by military jets during the September 11, 1973, military coup against President Salvador Allende. © AP Images.

"Do you have a US driver's license?' Mrs. Tipton asked me.

"Yes."

"Good," the Vice-Consul said. "Don't bother to come in today because we're about to close. But come in on Monday. Bring your license and ten dollars and we'll expedite you a new passport. Should take about a week, maybe ten days."

Stupefied, I argued with her. But to no avail. No special instructions to US citizens were being offered. "Just stay away from shooting and obey the new authorities," she said. As far as the Embassy was concerned, my predicament was a simple case of a lost passport.

They certainly knew better. But the political calculation had already been made. It was more important to give political support to the new dictatorship than it was to undermine its credibility by suggesting that American citizens needed protection against it.

Noon, Friday September 14

Turned away by the Embassy, I was now desperate. I rummaged through my mental Rolodex and focused on a long shot. An American friend of mine, an *Allendista* [supporter of Allende], had told me some months before that a guy named Dennis Allred, who served as the US Embassy's Student Affairs Counselor, was a decent man, a closet Allende sympathizer who took secret delight in handing out US scholarships to the most radical of Chilean students. True or not it seemed like the only chance I had.

I phoned the Embassy back. No, I was told, Mr. Allred wasn't in. But, yes, being a fellow American, I could have his home phone number. "Dennis, you don't know me," I told him after he answered his phone. "But I'm an American and I'm in trouble. I need . . ."

"OK," he said, cutting me short. "I don't care about the details. If you need a place to stay you're welcome here. Come now. I'm at Merced 280."

I thanked him and hung up. Merced 280? That would put him right next door to the heavily guarded US Consulate. Could I get past the troops? Patricia and I hurriedly made a plan. She would catch a bus to her parents' home but first would swing by my apartment and check its condition. She would call me later at Allred's. I would walk the seven miles to Allred's house as I had no ID and buses were being boarded and checked by soldiers.

My clothes were filthy. Melvin, who is 6' 2", lent me a pair of pants. I am 5' 3". I tucked the bottom of the pants up and pinned them inside with safety pins. He gave me a fresh shirt and I rolled the sleeves up over my wrists. On top of this unlikely outfit I wore my black leather jacket. For three hours I trudged toward Allred's house, protected only by sunglasses, taking side streets and looking far ahead for any checkpoints.

By 4 o'clock I was on the perimeter of the US Consulate. Neighboring Forestal Park was literally an armed camp. Armored carriers bristled with machine guns and helmeted troops. In front of the Consulate, a few steps from Dennis Allred's apartment, a company of soldiers lounged on a tank. I could hear my heart beating in my ears. I had no idea what I would tell the soldiers if challenged. I walked straight ahead, my eyes fixed on the door of Allred's building, my pace steady. Like passing through a time warp, I floated into the building uninterrupted.

A big, red-headed Bostoner, Allred greeted me alone in his luxury apartment. I was so pent up I could hardly talk at first. And then I began to talk too much. "I don't need to hear the details of your story. You can stay here as long as you have to," he said. He then offered me a tumbler full of Old Grandad [whiskey] which I gulped down like water. The booze took the edge off, and I slumped back in the broad padded mahogany chair. I called Patricia at her parents' house. I was relieved to hear that my apartment had not been raided. She had got in, picked up my passport and a couple hundred dollars, and tossed my .22 and the two boxes of ammo down a garbage chute. She would come and visit me the next day when the curfew was again to be lifted for a short time.

Over a real meal that evening—salad and Kraft macaroni and cheese—Allred told me the news, good and bad. "This apartment theoretically has diplomatic immunity, theoretically Chilean security cannot enter," he said. "On the other hand, the morning of the coup, the US Embassy took my passport, locked it in a safe, sent me home, and told me they'd call me when I should come back to work. So I don't know how much protection we really have." I could only guess that the stories my friend had told me about Allred were true.

That night, on the convertible bed in his den, the saddest of Portuguese *fadas* I had fished out of Allred's record collection drowned the sounds of sporadic gun fire and the rumble of tanks outside my window. With a strong sleeping pill Denis gave me I slept soundly for the first time in almost 100 hours. . . .

Noon, Monday September 17

Word had come that some Americans were missing. David Hathaway had been taken from his apartment. Frank Teruggi was unaccounted for. Sometime that day, our friend Charlie Horman would be seized. [All three were tortured and killed by the Pinochet Regime]. . . .

One young American professor rallied us in Allred's living room and we went as a delegation next door to speak to the US Consul. Enough was enough, we shouted. We wanted the US Embassy to do everything it could to find those who had been arrested. And we wanted protection for ourselves. We wanted the Americans to do what every other diplomatic delegation was doing in Chile—protecting its own citizens from a rampaging, barbarous military. The Consul, Frank Purdy, stood in the hall, blocking access to his office. He spouted the party line: he would look into these matters but there was nothing else to be done that day. The State Department had still issued no specific instructions for Americans in Chile. No special protection was to be extended.

"I recommend you be careful," Consul Purdy said. And then he looked us in the eye and came up with a straight-out lie. "The armed forces are restoring order but there's still a danger of scattered left-wing snipers. Be careful." With that he shooed us out of the Consulate. In retrospect we made mistakes. Our disgust with our government kept us from making what should have been the next logical move. We should have sat down and occupied the Consulate.

That afternoon, shortly after we slumped back from the meeting with the Consul, the whole apartment shook with a thud.

Then another bone-chilling thud. Walking out onto Allred's second-floor balcony we saw the two tanks that were doing the shelling. Comfortably squatting in the park, they lobbed artillery rounds into the Fine Arts Campus of the University of Chile across the river. That's how the armed forces of Chile were restoring order.

8 P.M., Tuesday September 18

One week since the coup, and the call came through from the Mexicans. Thanks to the Mexican government I was to be on a flight organized by the United Nations High Commissioner on Refugees for the next morning. Apart from a special military aircraft that carried Allende's widow to Mexico, this would be the first flight allowed out of Chile. There was a catch, of course. I had to be at the distant Sheraton Hotel the next morning at 7.30 sharp. But curfew didn't lift till 7. It was going to be tight. Nor could I get word to Patricia to meet me to say goodbye. She used a neighbor's phone and if I called her now, at night, it would be too dangerous to defy the curfew. I'd have to wait till morning to call. This was another low point. The mix of emotion I felt was paralyzing. I was ecstatic at the thought I might get out the next day, but terrified that something might go wrong. I was also deeply depressed, laden with survivor's guilt: my only prospect for joy was to flee the slaughterhouse of my friends.

7 A.M., Wednesday September 19

The moment the curfew lifted, I called Patricia and asked her to do what she could to meet me at the Sheraton. I hugged Allred goodbye. With only my passport, $200 in cash, and the borrowed clothes on my back, I walked past the encampment of soldiers outside Allred's door. On the corner, a daring taxi driver was ready for the post-curfew fares. When we got to the Sheraton, I began to reach into my pocket to pay him. The cabbie turned around and commenced one of those skilfully coded dialogues.

"Are you a foreigner?" he asked.

"Yes, an American."

"Have you been living in Chile?" he asked, noting my local accent.

"Yes, for nearly three years."

"Are you leaving today?"

"Yes. I am leaving."

"Then," the cabbie said, "there will be no charge. I want your thoughts about your last moments in Chile to be positive ones."

Operating on a emotional hair-trigger, I couldn't answer through my tears. I only nodded.

Inside the Sheraton lobby I was met by UN and Mexican officials. There was to be a motley mix of about fifty of us on this flight. Few of us knew each other. There were some Spanish clergy. Some Mexican teachers. An American researcher black and blue from a beating. A Texas high-school swim team that had had the bad luck to be passing through Santiago on the wrong day. Because Americans were on the flight manifest, American consular officials were there with clipboards in hand. We refused to talk to them.

Just before I boarded the bus to the airport Patricia arrived for a short goodbye—she would arrange to meet me later in the US. Under heavily armed military escort we were taken to the Cerrillos military airport. After bureaucratic stalling by the junta's new immigration officers, who challenged the validity of our UN-secured safe-conduct pass, we were herded onto a corporate 737 owned by LADECO, one of the copper companies nationalized by Allende.

There was an eerie silence as we took off. No one was sure of anyone else on the flight. As we gained altitude, the plane banked around and began to cross the majestic, snow-sparkled Andes en route to Buenos Aires. Twenty minutes into the flight a crackling voice came over the intercom. "Ladies and gentlemen," the captain announced crisply, "we have just entered Argentine air space."

The entire plane exploded into yelps of joy and applause. Soon we were all on our feet embracing each other, even the Texas swim team. The Kool-Aid and baloney sandwiches that were served remain to this day the best airplane meal I've ever had.

VIEWPOINT 2

A Foreign Worker Held in the National Stadium Concentration Camp

João

In the following viewpoint, a foreign worker describes his experiences being held prisoner in the Santiago, Chile, national stadium, which was used as a concentration camp, torture center, and place of execution during the first four years of Pinochet's regime. Although exact numbers are hard to establish, as many as 40,000 civilians were imprisoned for some period in the stadium, including roughly 1,800 known to have been executed there. The whereabouts of another 1,300 people who were imprisoned in the stadium continue to be unknown. The viewpoint was originally published in Sweden the year after the 1973 coup in Evidence on the Terror in Chile, *which collects more than a dozen first-person accounts from Chileans and foreign nationals swept up in the violence following the military coup.*

I was taken prisoner on the very same September 11th. At around midnight, due to my being a special case more or less, some two hundred soldiers arrived, well certainly a very large contingent, out of all proportion; I was taken to the barracks, it's

Raul Silva, Brigitta Leander, and Sun Axelsson, *Evidence on the Terror in Chile,* translated by Brian McBeth. London, UK: Merlin Press, 1974, pp. 16–23.

called the Telecommunications School of the Army. There were already several prisoners [there] (when I arrived). Myself and two other colleagues were taken to a room by mere chance one was another international official. He was a Colombian, and had also worked for the United Nations doing research on population problems; the other one was a Chilean. For a good part of the night they beat us. It lasted until nearly four o'clock in the morning. A prolonged beating, very violent, with a very brief interrogation. The impression we gained from the interrogation was that its purpose was nothing more than window dressing. I was not very coherent. This was until four o'clock, when they transferred us to the Police Station. Well, they treated us fairly well there, as one of the carabineros gave us the impression that he did not agree with the treatment accorded to the prisoners. So we were not beaten there. We received no food, at least in the section where I was being held as a prisoner. At seven in the morning of the 12th, the Army came back for us and took us once again to the barracks at the Telecommunication School of the Army, where the beatings continued, without any pretence of an interrogation. They were hitting people with rifle butts, without worrying too much about whether they would leave a mark or not; because, well, they thought they were the masters. Several times sham executions were held in those barracks. That . . . it lasted until five o'clock in the afternoon.

Arriving at the Stadium Concentration Camp

At five o'clock in the afternoon they transferred us by bus to the Chile Stadium [in Santiago]. Around forty prisoners were already there. When we arrived in front of the Chile Stadium, there is a sort of alleyway, a small passage where there is a very high wall of a building. It was there that the prisoners were being positioned, they were being placed in front of the wall. Well, as far as I could see there were hundreds of carabineros and troops . . . and well, they positioned the prisoners in front of the wall and started to beat them, to manhandle them; after that they forced the prisoners to enter the Chile Stadium. . . . they forced them (I don't know how you call it over here, a sort of 'Polish Corridor', a corridor that had a soldier at each side and one has to run the gauntlet in the middle, receiving blows). Well . . . there at the time that I went when they took me inside the Chile Stadium, there were around 1,500 prisoners outside. When we arrived inside, we were placed in a sort of hall, very large, where they would beat up the people before interrogating them. This was done by the Civil Police of Investigations. . . . This beating, in my own personal case was between 5 and 6 in the afternoon, the time I arrived until two o'clock in the morning, without interruption. They were always beating people without ever stopping, and the important fact was that, generally, it was done by officers including high ranking officers. I was even beaten by the Camp Commander, who was a Colonel whose name I forget now. I was subjected to continuous violence. Well, at around two o'clock in the morning, I do not have a clear idea of the time, I was very dizzy, they took me to a room for questioning. By the way they interrogated us they did not give us a chance to answer their questions properly. So that the questioning was carried out in a form that would elicit the answers that they wanted to hear. It was not an interrogation to obtain information, rather a type of self-incrimination. After the questioning we were taken to the stands inside the Stadium. When I arrived there were about 6,000 people. The Stadium's capacity is 40,000 people. There were people in the Stadium's stands. Each stand was guarded by some 50 soldiers. There were microphones that were used to call the prisoners to the torture chambers, installed in a sort of underground basement. The torture there was slightly more scientific. They were already using electric shocks and other instruments which do not leave much evidence of torture. People would enter the torture chamber in groups of ten or one by one. In the case of the Chileans, of the Chilean prisoners, there were hundreds who died of the blows they received from rifle butts.

There were above all, clearly outlined groups. Generally the ones with revolutionary views, belonging to MIR [the Revolutionary Left Movement] or to the Socialist Party: well, those were already doomed to die. Their torture was not to elicit information but only to kill them. In these cases, they did not use the torture chambers but the baths. Groups of between ten and fifteen would enter the baths. They would beat their heads in with their rifle butts until . . . well . . . until their heads were squashed. Later they would send soldiers to clean up. Although they cleaned up, one could still see evidence of the violence, because there was blood on the walls and at times even chunks of flesh that had been splattered by the . . . by the type of blow administered.

There were a series of corridors that took one to the torture chambers and also to the infirmary, here some of the tortured were taken. There were no doctors, only army medical orderlies. Sometimes we would feign any type of problem so as to get there and see, see which of our comrades were dying. At the side of this corridor there were heaps of corpses, which would later on be taken away by ambulances. All the time ambulances were leaving, transporting the bodies which they took out in stretchers, a sheet covering them, so that we could not see whether they were sick or dead. . . .

Executions in the Stadium Were Often Arbitrary

They killed many, but not the ones that they wanted to keep, because they could become potential informers. Well, inside the Stadium there was an atmosphere of immense terror, because . . . well, when they called people, even if they did not kill them, we had no way of knowing whether they were going to die or not. So great was the nervous tension, that many people went crazy, like a boy of 16 who became completely crazy. He would walk around the stadium and every-body knew that he was totally crazy. He said such things as: "Forgive me, God!" This boy had to be killed or silenced soon. One of the corridors was opened so that the

A few days after the military coup in 1973, a Chilean soldier stands guard over political prisoners held at the Chile National Stadium, which was used as a concentration camp to torture supporters of the ousted Marxist president Salvador Allende. © Bettmann/Corbis.

boy could enter. When he went in one of the soldiers took aim. The boy became frightened and started to shout and they shot him in front of 6,000 people. He died.

There was a protest. The people began to shout, and to calm down the situation the Camp Commander who was a Colonel ordered the soldiers to fire a volley of shots. They did not fire on the people, but at the walls. This lasted for five minutes and provoked a tremendous panic. There was the case of a worker who was pushed by the soldiers. He protested "There is no need to push, there is no reason for it". The soldier started to shout at him and later called the Camp Commander, saying that the worker had rebelled, that he had tried to get hold of his revolver. The Commander ordered two officers from the' special troops, called Black Berets, trained in Panama, to deal with him. They started to beat him up until he fell down, dead. When he had died, and was well dead—we saw it because we were very near to him—the Commander took out his pistol and fired at his head. There was a new protest and another firing volley. Six persons died.

I was in the Stadium from around five in the afternoon of Sept. 12th, until the Sunday afternoon of the 16th. One can not calculate the precise number of dead because the transportation of the corpses was a continuous one. The repression was much more violent on the MIR people; in general they were killed also with the workers from the factories, and later with members of the Socialist party. They considered them the most dangerous because they said they had a great number of fire-arms.

Highest Treatment Targets Young Chileans

They were also very violent with the young people because they felt that they were the most extreme revolutionaries. For example, in some factories, given the type of work, there were workers of 16, 17, 18 years of age. When they took over a factory, they would take everybody prisoner. I know of a factory where 400 people were taken prisoner. With relation to the foreigners, I can say that during the first moments, during the first few hours of the Stadium functioning as a concentration camp, the harshest beatings were given to the foreigners. Later on, during the tortures, they were harder on the Chileans, and it is a fact that they killed more Chileans. There were very few foreigners killed. For example, I was tortured for a long time, but they did not use electric shocks on me. Nevertheless they hit me with a sort of rubber truncheon with a steel cable inside, which does not leave any marks. It does not leave any marks, but it causes internal damage. Well, that was the principal thing that I had to contend with, although I also had some problems with my ribs. A comrade that was with me had two fractured ribs and has been without treatment until now, when they had started treating him. When those torture sessions finished, I could not walk or move. I was even taken to a seat in the stands where they had to help me sit down. I spent a day and a half without moving, without being able to move my head. But I did not suffer any torture on the feet. Generally speaking that was left to the Chileans. Also they did not strip me. The worst treatment afforded to the foreigners was in relation to food. I remained from the 12th to the 16th without receiving any type of food, the only thing they gave me one day was an eighth of a loaf of bread, one loaf for eight people, everybody in the stadium except the foreigners received this ration.

There was one comrade who jumped from one of the high stands after he shouted "Death to the fascist murderers!" He fell on one of the lower stands and remained unconscious, but recovered soon although he was wounded and remained lying down. Some Black Beret officers arrived, and took him away; two held his feet, picking him up in a vertical position, so that the feet could not touch the ground. Two took him this way while two others administered rifle butt blows on his face. They took him across the stadium in this manner, and when they arrived at the stairs, the stairs that led to the torture chambers, he was dead. He was dead from all the blows that he had received on his face. The Camp Commander shot him in the head.

There was another comrade who stood up and shouted "Down with Fascism!" The Commander asked, "Who was that?" Then he stood up again and said: "I did". The Commander ordered: "Come over here". The comrade slowly started to walk over, very calm; when he reached the stairs he received a shot in the neck.

There were cases in which twelve people died, some of them very young; two of them must have been between 16 and 17 years old. That group was taken to one of the baths, stripped and beaten to death. Their moans could be heard all over the Stadium. These sessions lasted, in general, fifteen to twenty minutes, they took such a violent form that in 15 to 20 minutes one could die. After these sessions in the baths, a team of soldiers would clean up, so as to clear up the evidence of blood. After this cleaning up job, the Chileans generally had free access to the Stadium. At one point, one of the Chileans whom I had known before, called me to have a look. I went down to the basement with the excuse of going to the infirmary, and in a corridor I noticed around 6 naked bodies that were mutilated by bayonets, waiting to be transported out by ambulance.

Living Conditions Cause Madness

There was a worker who went mad and started to shout meaningless words. He shouted things like "Please forgive me; my Colonel, my only fault was to drink a little bit too much". He became very troublesome and had to be taken away. He was given an injection but he immediately recovered and once again started to scream. He was then tied to a stretcher and taken to a room in one of the stands, equipped with an infirmary and given another injection. They left him alone as they thought he was sleeping. But once again he recovered and this time came out running and flung himself from the stands falling on to the playing field. He remained there for a few minutes unconscious, then he got up and flung himself against. . . . how do you call them—a colon?—a column, he ran head first at the front of the column and fell unconscious. They took him out to the basement and on the stairs they shot him.

Another thing that added to the general condition of the Chile Stadium was that sleep was impossible. Apart from the tension, hunger (four died of thirst), one could not sleep, firstly, because of the nervous tension, and secondly because of the noise that the tortured prisoners made. To this must be added the fact that we were seated in the stands or in the playing fields, very close together and without being able to move. A moment was reached when the people were so tired that even the soldiers were affected by it; reaching such a level that the Camp

Commander had to take the microphone and speak of the need to be calm and that the people should not be afraid; that he was going to read out a newspaper so as to distract them, the third edition of *La Hora de Santiago*. The people were so nervous and perturbed that when he finished reading, they applauded him. It was a form of protest, the only one that was allowed.

Viewpoint 3

The Systemic Sexual Torture of Chilean Women

Róbinson Rojas Sandford

The following viewpoint is an excerpt from The Murder of Allende and the End of the Chilean Way of Socialism, *a brief account of the conditions endured by women arrested under Augusto Pinochet's regime. Testimonies from anonymous survivors, taken soon after their release, highlight the frequent and systematic use of sexual degradation, assault, and torture before and during interrogations. The viewpoint also describes how this mistreatment was integrated into the daily life of women who were at odds with authorities. Róbinson Rojas Sandford has taught at Open University and the University of East London and has consulted for the BBC World Service. His books include* Yankee Imperialism in Chile and Latin America: Blockages to Development. *He maintains the Róbinson Rojas Archives website, a clearinghouse for information about economic and development issues in Chile, People's Republic of China, Taiwan, Latin America, Southeast Asia, and East Asia.*

The military torture teams, graduates of the Americas School in the Canal Zone, have revealed a degree of human bes-

Excerpt from pp. 206–207 [500 words] *from The Murder of Allende and the End of the Chilean Way to Socialism* by Róbinson Rojas Sandford and translated by Andre Conrad.

tiality with Chilean women that puts them way ahead of their American Trainers.

The Treatment of Women Held in the National Stadium

A woman professor at the East Santiago campus of the University of Chile, married, with two children, was detained for forty days in the National Stadium. She wrote me this about the "female prisoners of war":

> They were obliged to remain all day long face down with their hands on their necks and their legs spread. . . . There were lines of them kneeling or standing against the walls, and at the slightest movement they were struck or kicked—and, in several cases I saw, shot. In rooms fifteen by eighteen feet [4.5m by 5.5m] there were a hundred women. Food came, only once a day, at 4 or 5 P.M. There were mainly two groups or women: workers and university professors. Girls and women were harassed, obliged to disrobe, manhandled, and insulted as a preamble to the interrogations. The academics among us had been taken out of our classrooms at gunpoint. One group of schoolteachers had a typically sad experience: at the investigatory commission one of them had her hair cropped off . . . then at Los Cerros de Chena [a concentration camp at a Chilean air force base near the city of San Bernardo], the eyes were always blindfolded. To go to the bathroom, they had to be accompanied by guards who took the opportunity to manhandle and beat them. They were interrogated naked. Electric current was applied to the mouth, hands, nipples, vagina. Water was poured over their bodies to intensify the pain. The language used with them was completely degenerate; they were forced to repeat, over and over: "I am a cunt, I am a cunt. . . ." A hospital technician was taken to the Quinta Normal naval enclosure. She was kept there for three days without sleep, and subjected to electric tortures every few hours. She also had electricity applied to her vagina. Afterward they brought her to the National Stadium. She was taken for interrogation there too,

> blindfolded as others were. This time she apparently was taken to the cycle track, where by then the torture chamber had been installed. Besides electric shocks, this time she was forced to take something in her hand. They had given her an injection, which she guessed was Sodium Pentothal, and it had made her dizzy, but she was still conscious. At once she realized the object was a penis which, on contact with her hand, became erect. They thrust it into her mouth, where it ejaculated.

Frequent Sexual Assaults

I have other memoranda from women prisoners who were able to write to me afterward. Essentially they tell the same story, although they add that some officials would intimate that there were "hard methods of interrogation" to "soften," "extract information," and "morally intimidate."

Some novelties appear in those memoranda: "They stretched the women out on tables and dripped candle wax on their stomachs." "There were rapes, either in groups or individually. 'Move, you Marxist whore,' they would tell the victims. 'If you don't respond you're going to have to suck cock, even for General Pinochet, you shitty whore.'" "Some officers started by sticking their fingers in my vagina, hoping to excite me. . . ."

There are plenty of examples; the newspapers of the world are filled with them. The cemeteries of Chile are filled with mutilated corpses.

Viewpoint 4

The "Disappearance" of Carlos Fariña Oyarce, Age 13

Amnesty International

The following viewpoint excerpts a 2001 report that included a selection of case studies culled from more than one thousand documented "disappearances" recognized by Patricio Aylwin, the first president elected in Chile with the restoration of democracy in 1990. Desaparecidos, *or "disappeared," is a term applied to citizens who were arrested by the police or military (or individuals claiming to be police or military) and never heard from again. It is unknown how many Chileans were "disappeared" under Pinochet, why they were arrested, where they were held, how long they suffered, how they died, or where their bodies were disposed. These unresolved questions—and the slim possibility that some of the disappeared are still alive—have created immeasurable psychological duress for the families of those lost and for the Chilean people as a whole. Amnesty International is a global organization dedicated to protecting and expanding human rights throughout the world.*

In June 2000, 27 years after he was taken from his home by members of the security forces, the remains of Carlos Fariña

Amnesty International, *Chile: Testament to Suffering and Courage: The Long Quest for Justice and Truth,* AMR 22/014/2001. London, UK: Amnesty International Publications, December 10, 2011.

Oyarce were uncovered by construction workers on wasteland in the western part of Santiago [Chile]. He was 13 years old at the time of his abduction and is the youngest of the "disappeared" prisoners of Chile. According to his brothers, his body bore the signs of 12 gunshot wounds—four in the head and eight in the back. His mother, Josefina Oyarce died from cancer in 1977 before her son's remains were located.

The Arrest of a Thirteen-Year-Old Boy

Carlos Fariña Oyarce was detained on 13 October 1973 by members of the Yungay army regiment of San Felipe, *Carabineros* (uniformed police) and *Investigaciones* (criminal investigations police) who entered the family home in Conchalí 'on the outskirts of Santiago at about 10 in the morning. The men asked for Carlos to be handed over. Two of the *Carabineros* pulled him out of bed and one of them hit him hard in the chest with a rifle butt causing Carlos to fall over. According to his mother's testimony, he was practically dragged out of the house and taken to the local football field where other people who lived in the area had been rounded up by the security forces. His mother pleaded with the officer in charge of the troops to let her son go because he was ill but was told that he would be handed back when he was grown up. Carlos Fariña was subsequently driven away in a military jeep by two soldiers and taken to an unknown destination.

Shortly before his arrest, Carlos Fariña had been involved in an incident in which a young neighbour had accidentally been wounded with a gun that Carlos had been looking after for a local older boy. The neighbour's mother went to the local police station to denounce the incident. On discovering what happened and on the advice of the police, Carlos Fariña's mother took him to the local youth court. The court ordered him to be sent to a Youth Detention Centre but the child ran away after apparently being sexually abused. He arrived home with a high temperature and his mother decided to wait for him to get better before tell-

Our lives, my life, changed dramatically after the coup, that's why this is so personal. My wife was five months pregnant when arrested by a special secret police unit. Where were the now-vociferous Pinochet supporters when she was sent to a men's prison and kept in solitary confinement? Did they ever think about the suffering of our baby? He was born with mild brain damage, but of course the rich politicians, businessmen and lawyers who complain about the treatment of Pinochet never helped him.

It's also personal because we had to endure many years in exile, because our children were born abroad and then went back to Chile to live out their own exile. Ireland was a place of refuge, but it was never home. We lived in England, but it was never home. It was exile, that slow and painful way of withering away from your family, friends, past and present. Above all it was the realisation that you were not part of your country's future. So we came back, but the military had changed the country's trees and lakes, they had moved the mountains and the sea. Nothing was the same.

But nothing mattered, because we were home at last. We were happy, until the night the secret police broke into the tranquility of our home, ransacking the place, stealing the little we had and shattering the peace of the neighbourhood. Nothing had changed.

They terrorized my pregnant wife and the little being in her womb. "It is war", they shouted, before ripping away my clothes, tying my hands behind my back and putting a hood over my head. They took turns in beating me up, I could feel their stale breath, their joy when their fists or kicks met the flesh. I stood there, naked, tied up, blindfolded and defenceless, but proud.

Yes, proud, because I was better than they were, because I had nothing to be ashamed of. What do they know about ideals, ethics or morality, they who have been trained in the "art" of killing? They were the raving animals while I was more humane than ever before, conquering fear in the name of freedom.

People celebrate with champagne in the streets of Santiago, Chile, in October 1999 upon hearing the news that former dictator Augusto Pinochet will be extradited to Spain to face allegations of crimes against humanity. © Sinead Lynch/AFP/Getty Images.

The pain rushed through my entire body, it got increasingly hot in that room, the torture session went on forever. Was it still night-time, was the sun already coming out, were people leaving their homes to work, were little children going to school unaware that in a dark basement cell yet another human being was being tortured by a group of cowards?

I will never know the answer to these questions. All I know is that at one point I was taken to another room, tied to a chair, threatened with being executed before tiny electrodes were fixed to my wrists and genitals. It was electricity. You could feel it coming, travelling throughout your body like a million pins pinching your flesh, your bones, your kidneys, and your brain. It is a painful explosion of shiny colours that comes out of your mouth in the form of a scream that you cannot control. It is as if somebody else is screaming in the room; it is not your scream, it is not your body, but it is your pain. You swallow electricity and you vomit electricity. It hurts, and they know it. That is why this is personal.

I spent four months with a plaster cast from my neck to my waist because they broke my back. Not in a private clinic, not in a hospital, but in prison. Because ten years went by before I could get a job, because my first wife died without knowing what true democracy is. Because I was separated from my children and it hurt.

President Eduardo Frei has called upon the Chilean people to remain calm. But, you know what? I don't want to remain calm, for this is personal, this is between Pinochet and I. I want the whole world to know that he is a murderer, a terrorist, a criminal, an animal. I want the whole world to know that I feel deeply embarrassed by the civilian government's defence of the dictator. It sickens me that two European countries have finally arrested Pinochet, because our own judicial system was unable or unwilling to bring him to justice.

I don't care whether he is 80 or 100 years old. He must pay for his horrendous crimes. We will never rest until he and all those responsible for crimes against our people are brought to justice. It is not only a legal or political problem, it's personal, because I was lucky, because I survived, because it is my duty to pay homage to all my sisters and brothers who fell in the struggle against the dictatorship.

Organizations to Contact

The editors have compiled the following list of organizations concerned with the issues debated in this book. The descriptions are derived from materials provided by the organizations. All have publications or information available for interested readers. The list was compiled on the date of publication of the present volume; the information provided here may change. Be aware that many organizations take several weeks or longer to respond to inquiries, so allow as much time as possible.

Amnesty International
5 Penn Plaza, 14th Floor
New York, NY 10001
(212) 807-8400 • fax: (212) 463-9193
email: aimember@aiusa.org
website: www.amnestyusa.org

Amnesty International is a worldwide campaign for internationally recognized human rights and a world in which every person enjoys all of the rights enshrined in the Universal Declaration of Human Rights. Their website contains several articles on Chile, an annual report on human rights conditions in Chile, and other documents including "Chile: Reports of Torture since March 1990," "Chile: Five Cases of Torture and Ill-treatment," and "'Disappearances' and Political Killings: Human Rights Crisis of the 1990s—A Manual for Action."

Genocide Watch
PO Box 809
Washington, DC 20044
(202) 643-1405
email: communications@genocidewatch.org
website: www.genocidewatch.org

Genocide Watch's mission is to "predict, prevent, stop, and punish genocide and other forms of mass murder" by raising awareness of the eight-stage process of genocide and by influencing international policy to curtail potential and actual acts of genocide. Their website includes news alerts and annual reports on countries at risk due to a growing likelihood of genocide or other atrocities. The website also offers links to reports issued by other members of the International Alliance to End Genocide, an international coalition of similar organizations coordinated through Genocide Watch.

Human Rights International Project

PO Box 32776
London SE1 1AX
United Kingdom
email: info@memoriaviva.com
website: www.memoriaviva.com

The Human Rights International Project is a nongovernmental organization founded by Chilean expatriates living in London. The project works to assure political and personal accountability for atrocities committed within Chile. Their primary goal is to gather, archive, and publish information pertaining to human rights abuses associated with Augusto Pinochet's regime. They also published several hundred issues of the Spanish-language *Human Rights Bulletin—Chile,* which tracked ongoing human rights issues in the nation.

Human Rights Watch

350 Fifth Avenue, 34th Floor
New York, NY 10118-3299
(212) 290-4700 • fax: (212) 736-1300
email: hrwnyc@hrw.org
website: www.hrw.org

Founded in 1978, this nongovernmental organization conducts systematic investigations of human rights abuses around the world and actively advocates for human dignity. Human Rights Watch (HRW) publishes many books and reports on specific countries and issues, as well as annual reports and other articles. Its website includes numerous discussions of human rights and international justice issues, including coverage of ongoing human rights problems in Chile, specifically those targeting the Mapuche indigenous community.

Montreal Institute for Genocide and Human Rights Studies

Concordia University
1455 De Maisonneuve Blvd.
West Montreal, Quebec H3G 1M8 Canada
(514) 848-2424, ext. 5729 or 2404 • fax: (514) 848-4538
website: http://migs.concordia.ca

Founded in 1986, the Montreal Institute for Genocide and Human Rights Studies (MIGS) monitors native-language media for early warning signs of genocide in countries deemed to be at risk of mass atrocities. The institute houses the Will to Intervene Project, a research initiative focused on the prevention of genocide and other mass atrocities. The institute also collects and disseminates research on the historical origins of mass killings and provides comprehensive links to this and other research materials on its website.

STAND/United to End Genocide

1025 Connecticut Avenue, Suite 310
Washington, DC 20036
(202) 556-2100
email: info@standnow.org
website: www.standnow.org

STAND is the student-led division of United to End Genocide (formerly Genocide Intervention Network). STAND envisions a world in which the global community is willing and able to protect civilians from genocide and mass atrocities. In order to empower individuals and communities with the tools to prevent and stop genocide, STAND recommends activities from engaging government representatives to hosting fundraisers, and it has more than a thousand student chapters at colleges and high schools. STAND maintains many documents and other online resources and also provides plans for promoting action and education.

United Human Rights Council (UHRC)

104 N. Belmont Street, Suite 313
Glendale, CA 91206
(818) 507-1933
website: www.unitedhumanrights.org

The United Human Rights Council (UHRC) is a committee of the Armenian Youth Federation. UHRC uses grassroots action to work toward exposing and correcting human rights violations by governments worldwide. The UHRC campaigns against violators in an effort to generate awareness through boycotts, community outreach, and education. The UHRC website focuses on genocides of the twentieth century.

List of Primary Source Documents

The editors have compiled the following list of documents that either broadly address genocide and persecution or more narrowly focus on the topic of this volume. The full text of these documents is available from multiple sources in print and online.

Convention Against Torture and Other Cruel, Inhuman, or Degrading Punishment, United Nations, 1974

This document was a draft resolution adopted by the United Nations General Assembly in 1974 opposing any nation's use of torture, unusually harsh punishment, or unfair imprisonment.

Convention on the Prevention and Punishment of the Crime of Genocide, December 9, 1948

This resolution of the United Nations General Assembly defines genocide in legal terms and advises participating countries to prevent and punish actions of genocide in war and peacetime.

The National Commission on Political Imprisonment and Torture Report ("Valech Report"), November 29, 2004 (revised June 1, 2005)

This report resulted from a six-month investigation by the National Commission on Political Imprisonment and Torture. Bishop Sergio Valech headed the commission at the request of Chilean President Ricardo Lagos, one of Augusto Pinochet's principal opponents during the 1988 plebiscite that led to Pinochet leaving office. The initial report was based on testimony from 35,865 people, of which almost 80 percent were determined to have been tortured. The commission was later reopened to examine another 32,000 cases, from which an additional 9,825 incidents of torture, execution, or disappearance were certified.

The National Commission for Truth and Reconciliation Report ("Rettig Report"), February 1991

This report was produced by Chile's National Commission for Truth and Reconciliation at the behest of Patricio Aylwin, Chile's first democratically elected president following Augusto Pinochet's rule. The commission was headed by Raúl Rettig, a former Chilean ambassador under Salvador Allende. The Rettig Report shows that 2,279 people were killed for political reasons during Pinochet's regime (including 957 "disappeared" individuals presumed to be dead).

Principles of International Law Recognized in the Charter of the Nuremberg Tribunal, United Nations International Law Commission, 1950

After World War II (1939–1945) the victorious allies legally tried surviving leaders of Nazi Germany in the German city of Nuremberg. The proceedings established standards for international law that were affirmed by the United Nations and by later court tests. Among other standards, national leaders can be held responsible for crimes against humanity, which might include "murder, extermination, deportation, enslavement, and other inhuman acts."

Rome Statute of the International Criminal Court, July 17, 1998

This treaty establishes the International Criminal Court. It outlines the court's functions, jurisdiction, and structure.

United Nations General Assembly, Resolution 96 on the Crime of Genocide, December 11, 1946

This resolution of the United Nations General Assembly affirms that genocide is a crime under international law.

United Nations General Assembly, Resolution 32/118 on "Protection of Human Rights in Chile," December 16, 1977

The fourth resolution on "flagrant violations of human rights" in Chile, this document represents the first time the United Nations General Assembly acknowledged the full breadth of ongoing abuses in Chile, including the "disappearing" of citizens for political reasons. The United Nations would go on to affirm similarly worded resolutions for the next decade.

Universal Declaration of Human Rights, United Nations, 1948

Soon after its founding, the United Nations approved this general statement of individual rights it hoped would apply to citizens of all nations.

Whitaker Report on Genocide, 1985

This report addresses the question of the prevention and punishment of the crime of genocide. It calls for the establishment of an international criminal court and a system of universal jurisdiction to ensure that genocide is punished.

For Further Research

Books

Jerome R. Adams, *Liberators, Patriots, and Leaders of Latin America: 32 Biographies*, 2nd ed. Jefferson, NC: McFarland, 2010.

Genaro Arriagada, *Pinochet: The Politics of Power.* Boston: Unwin Hyman, 1988.

Pamela Constable and Arturo Valenzuela. *A Nation of Enemies: Chile Under Pinochet*. New York: W.W. Norton and Company, 1993.

John Dinges, *The Condor Years: How Pinochet and His Allies Brought Terrorism to Three Continents*. New York: The New Press, 2005.

Mark Ensalaco, *Chile Under Pinochet: Recovering the Truth*. Philadelphia: University of Pennsylvania Press, 1999.

Peter Kornbluh, *The Pinochet File: A Declassified Dossier on Atrocity and Accountability.* New York: The New Press, 2003.

Hugh O'Shaughnessy, *Pinochet: The Politics of Torture*. London: Central Books, 1999.

Naomi Roht-Arriaza, *The Pinochet Effect: Transnational Justice in the Age of Human Rights*. Philadelphia: University of Pennsylvania Press, 2006.

Jacobo Timerman, *Chile: Death in the South*. New York: Knopf, 1987.

Patricia Verdugo, *Chile, Pinochet, and the Caravan of Death,* translated by Marcelo Montecino. Coral Gables, FL: University of Miami North-South Center Press, 2001.

James R. Whelan, *Out of the Ashes: Life, Death, and Transfiguration of Democracy in Chile, 1833–1988*. Washington: Regnery, 1989.

Periodicals and Internet Sources

"Augusto Pinochet and the Realities of the Free Market in Chile," *The Red Phoenix*, May 27, 2011. http://theredphoenixapl.org.

William J. Barber, "Chile con Chicago: A Review Essay," *Journal of Economic Literature*, vol. 23, December 1995.

Gary S. Becker, "Latin America Owes a Lot to Its 'Chicago Boys,'" *Business Week*, June 9, 1997. http://home.uchicago.edu/~gbecker.

Andrew Buncombe, "The Pinochet Affair: 'I Saw Them Herded to Their Death. I Heard the Gunfire as They Died,'" *The Independent*, October 21, 1998. www.independent.co.uk.

Roger Burbach, "Pinochet's Trial and Tribulations," *Z Magazine*, May 2000.

"Chile: Progress and Its Discontents," *The Economist*, April 14, 2012. www.economist.com.

Tyler Cowen, "How Good Was Pinochet for the Chilean Economy?," *Marginal Revolution*, December 20, 2006. http://marginalrevolution.com.

"A Dictator's Double Standard," *Washington Post*, December 12, 2006. www.washingtonpost.com.

Bruce Falconer, "The Torture Colony," *American Scholar*, Autumn 2008. http://theamericanscholar.org.

Eduardo Gallardo, "In Letter, Pinochet Called Abuses in Chile 'Necessary,'" *Washington Post*, December 25, 2006. www.washingtonpost.com.

Steven Gimbel, "Death and the Chilean Miracle," *Philosophers' Playground*, December 15, 2006. http://philosophersplayground.blogspot.com.

Jonah Goldberg, "Iraq Needs a Pinochet," *Los Angeles Times*, December 14, 2006. www.latimes.com.

Government of Chile, Ministry of Housing and Urban Development, "Valech Report: Never to Be Lived Again, Never to Be Denied Again," October 2006. www.minvu.cl.

Barbara Harff, "No Lessons Learned from the Holocaust? Assessing Risks of Genocide and Political Mass Murder since 1955," *American Political Science Review*, vol. 97, no. 1, February 2003.

Human Rights Watch, "Chile: Government Discloses Torture Was State Policy," November 30, 2004. www.hrw.org.

Jeane J. Kirkpatrick, "Dictatorships and Double Standards," *Commentary*, November 1, 1979. www.commentarymaga zine.com.

Jennifer Koduru, "Situation of Mapuche Children in Chile," *Human Rights Brief*, March 26, 2011. http://hrbrief.org.

Peter Kornbluh, "Chile Declassified," *The Nation*, July 22, 1999. www.thenation.com.

Peter Kornbluh, "CIA Outrages in Chile," *The Nation*, October 16, 2000. www.thenation.com.

Peter Kornbluh, "Kissinger and Pinochet," *The Nation*, March 29, 1999. www.thenation.com.

PBS/WGBH, "Milton Friedman," *Commanding Heights: The Battle for the World Economy*, October 1, 2000. www.pbs .org.

Greg Palast, "Tinker Bell, Pinochet, and the Fairy Tale Miracle of Chile," *ZNet*, December 13, 2006. December 13, 2006. www.gregpalast.com.

"Pinochet 'Innocent' of Death Squad Crimes," BBC News, July 20, 2000. http://news.bbc.co.uk.

"Pinochet 'Takes Responsibility,'" BBC News, November 25, 2006. http://news.bbc.co.uk.

Websites and Films

Chile Documentation Project, The National Security Archive (www.gwu.edu/~nsarchiv/latin_america/chile.htm). The National Security Archive is a nongovernmental nonprofit research institution associated with George Washington University in Washington, DC. They unearth, archive, and publish declassified documents associated with US foreign policy. Their Chile Documentation Project specifically focuses on US involvement with and support of Pinochet's regime.

Death and the Maiden (1994). Roman Polanski directed this film adaptation of Chilean author Ariel Dorfman's 1990 play of the same name. The story is set in an unnamed Latin American country several years after the fall of a dictatorship closely resembling Pinochet's in Chile. It involves a woman who holds a suspected former torturer hostage and subjects him to a mock trial.

Memoria Viva (www.memoriaviva.com). This website is the Human Rights International Project's digital archive of documents and testimony related to human rights violations committed by Chile's military dictatorship between 1973 and 1990. It currently hosts more than eight thousand pages of evidence and testimony (many translated into English at www.memoriaviva.com/english.htm).

Puro Chile: The Memory of the People (www.purochile.rrojas databank.info). This website is dedicated "to those who fell, were tortured, to those who disappeared, were killed, to those who were humiliated and offended by the monstrous claw of the murderers in uniform." It is part of the Róbinson Rojas Archive, a website is maintained by Róbinson Rojas Sandford, an educator and researcher specializing in Asian and Latin American economic and development issues.